RIDE GUIDE

Central Jersey

2nd Edition

by Dan Goldfischer

RIDE GUIDE Central Jersey - 2nd Edition
Copyright 1999 by Daniel Goldfischer

Cover: *photo by Albert Knight; design by Jean Sullivan*

Maps: *Richard Widhu*

ISBN: 0-933855-18-4
Library of Congress Catalog Card Number: 99-72208

Also available:
Bed, Breakfast & Bike Mid-Atlantic
Bed, Breakfast & Bike Pacific Northwest
RIDE GUIDE New Jersey Mountain Biking
RIDE GUIDE Mountain Biking in the New York Metro Area
RIDE GUIDE North Jersey 2nd Edition
RIDE GUIDE South Jersey 2nd Edition
RIDE GUIDE Hudson Valley New Paltz to Staten Island 2nd Edition
Please send for our catalog

Published by

ANACUS PRESS INC.

P.O. Box 4544, Warren, New Jersey 07059

*"Ride Guide" and "Bed, Breakfast and Bike"
are trademarks of Anacus Press, Inc.*

Printed in the United States of America

ACKNOWLEDGMENTS

Thanks once again to my wife Sharlene, son Eric, and daughter Amy for their love and patience as once again I took to the road to check on my favorite recreational pastime.

And thanks to Anacus Press for keeping the RIDE GUIDE nameplate alive, well, and thriving.

CONTENTS

Preface... 7
Before You Go.. 9
How To Use This Book... 11
Starting Points Map... 15

RIDES STARTING IN SOMERSET COUNTY.................... 17
Far Hills Dirt Road Special *HYBRID* (26.0 miles).............. 19
Far Hills-Washington Rock (29.5 miles)........................ 25
Far Hills-Oldwick (31.7 miles).................................... 29
Somerset Rivers Ride (42.1 miles)............................... 35
The New Flat Century (102.9 miles).............................. 41

RIDES STARTING IN HUNTERDON COUNTY.................... 47
Clinton-Pittstown *HYBRID* (24.2 miles)......................... 49
Bloomsbury-Riegelsville (27.1 miles)............................ 55
Tewksbury-Hacklebarney (30.0 miles)........................... 59
Northern Hunterdon Hillbilly (30.0 miles)........................ 63
South Brancher (31.4 miles)...................................... 67
Round The Valley (39.6 miles).................................... 73
Flemington-Raven Rock (39.8 miles).............................. 77

**RIDES STARTING IN MIDDLESEX, MONMOUTH,
AND OCEAN COUNTIES**.. 83
Manalapan-Millstone (28.0 miles)................................ 85
Highland Park-Griggstown *HYBRID* (29.7 miles)............... 89
Allaire-Ocean Grove (33.3 miles)................................. 93
Cheesequake-Englishtown (39.4 miles)........................... 99
Allaire-Lakewood (40.3 miles).................................... 103
Island Beach-Point Pleasant (41.4 miles)....................... 109
Lincroft-Sandy Hook (43.0 miles)................................ 115
Freehold-Colts Neck (43.9 miles)................................ 121
Sandy Hook Express *HYBRID* (43.9 miles)...................... 125
Cheesequake-Sandy Hook (61.4 miles)........................... 133

RIDES STARTING IN MERCER COUNTY.......................... 139
Princeton Canalier Ride (40.8 miles)............................. 141
Princeton-Crosswicks (47.5 miles)............................... 147
Princeton-Stockton (55.1 miles).................................. 151
Princeton-Englishtown (56.8 miles).............................. 159

Two things that will help you get the most out of this RIDE GUIDE*: a hybrid and a helmet. The former will help you conquer the four routes that venture off the pavement, and the latter will protect your head if you spill. Shown here at Washington Rock, overlooking the Plainfield area.*

PREFACE

In 1989, spurred by the popularity of its original volume, *RIDE GUIDE for North Jersey and Beyond*, White Meadow Press (now Anacus Press) split the book into two: *RIDE GUIDE/North Jersey* and *RIDE GUIDE/Central Jersey*.

In the ensuing decade, the North Jersey book gained a new edition and a reduced size, enabling cyclists to once again fit the volume in their handlebar bags (the original book was also small-sized). Bicycle stores in Central Jersey wanted equal treatment: They wanted to sell a quality book of handlebar-bag size that included some off-road rides.

At long last, that book is here: *RIDE GUIDE/Central Jersey 2nd Edition*. Each time I research a revised book, I brace myself for the inevitable loss of prime cycling roads to development, heavy traffic, and so-called "progress."

I am happy to report that although Central Jersey certainly has grown (especially in the areas around Princeton, Freehold and New Brunswick), I did not have to drop a single ride from the 1989 edition. Revisions were necessary to take into account changing road patterns, stores that have gone out of business, and new stores that have opened, but all 21 routes of the original book are still here.

The beauty of this edition is that there are five new routes, and four of them—designated "hybrid"—are especially for owners of fat-tired bikes. These unusual routes are not all-trail mountain bike routes (those can be found in the companion Anacus Press guidebook *RIDE GUIDE/New Jersey Mountain Biking*), but combination road and dirt routes.

Some of the new routes feature unpaved roads, such as Far Hills Dirt Road Special. This type of route can't be found in any other guidebook. It provides an exhilarating day of riding in countryside that thin-tired cyclists probably didn't know existed. Other routes travel on the hard-packed dirt of easier All Terrain Bicycle trails, such as Highland Park-Griggstown which visits the Delaware & Raritan Canal towpath, and combines them with road riding to prevent the boring "out-and-back" type ride that one often encounters on linear trails.

The countryside is still beautiful in Central Jersey, despite the growth. From hilly Hunterdon County, along the sleepy Delaware River, down through the Millstone Valley, out from Princeton in four directions, and over to the Jersey Shore: Come out and ride! Enjoy, and bring the new *RIDE GUIDE/ Central Jersey* along.

BEFORE YOU GO

The beauty of cycling is that it is a simple sport. You don't have to be as concerned about equipment as with sports like boating or scuba diving. And thanks to *RIDE GUIDE*, you don't have to travel far to enjoy good routes.

However, some simple pre-ride preparation will make your bike tour more enjoyable. Check the weather report and dress accordingly: If it's below 60 degrees when you start off, most sports medicine experts recommend wearing long sweatpants or cycling tights. If it's supposed to warm up, change into shorts (or peel off the tights you wore over your bike shorts). It might be a good idea to pack a rain jacket in a handlebar- or rack-top bag just in case. Ponchos and cycling don't mix, due to the possibility of chain or wheel entanglement.

Speaking of keeping things out of the chain, novice riders might take a few hints from intermediates and use trouser clips to prevent flapping or greasy pant legs. Also, double-knot your shoelaces and tuck them into the shoe—we've seen a few crashes due to excess lace length reaching the front changer or getting caught between the chain and chainwheel.

Be sure to bring plenty of water. Sip from your bottle every 10 minutes or so, because cycling takes quite a bit of fluid out of you, even when it's cool out. Also, take along snacks such as bananas or fig bars. Most of our routes have deli stops, but some may not be for the first 20 miles, so you might want to be prepared for early hunger pangs with some fruit, gorp, or cookies.

Basic tools such as tire irons, a frame pump, patch kit, screw driver, Allen wrenches and the like (and knowledge of how to use them) are necessary for the well-prepared cyclist. Most local bike clubs hold clinics on repairing flat tires, adjusting derailleurs, replacing broken cables and fixing other things that might go wrong on the road. May you never have to use this knowledge, but it's always good to have, just in case.

On certain routes, carrying insect repellent is a good idea. This is especially true when traveling on dirt roads between June and September, or if the lunch spot is a woodsy park. Also, watch out for poison ivy. That pleasant-looking three-leaved vine climbing the tree on which your bike is leaning may give you a rash later. It grows in profusion on roads bordering farm fields.

By the way, those changes in elevation that occur in certain parts of Central Jersey should not be put in the same category as insects. Hills are challenges that actually make the ride more fun, because you get to ride down them! Don't let hills discourage you, especially if you are a novice rider. Walk if you have to, take your time and look at the scenery, and enjoy the downhill run and the view. Toe clips or straps will vastly increase your power cycling uphill, and are worth the investment

Of course, selection of the bike is an important preparation step. Even in Central Jersey, which for the most part is less hilly than North Jersey, a bike with a "granny gear" (third chainring) is a good idea. That low chainring will give you the ability to climb walls, such as the ascent to Twin Lights near Sandy Hook.

The width of your tires should depend on whether the route is designated "hybrid." Those routes require a hybrid or all-terrain bicycle with fat tires to handle a good amount of unpaved roads or paths. All other routes can be ridden by any type of bicycle—thin- or fat-tired.

Finally, you should not ride without your life insurance—an ANSI-approved, Snell-rated helmet. There have been a number of instances in the last few years where this simple item has made the difference between a crashing rider becoming a vegetable, or a statistic, or remaining around to cycle many more New Jersey roads in good health. The newest helmets are made of incredibly lightweight polystyrene or other plastics, and you don't even realize you have it on. Invest in a helmet and then use it!

Have a happy, safe tour and thanks for using *RIDE GUIDE.*

HOW TO USE THIS BOOK

RIDE GUIDE/Central Jersey is organized into four sections according to the county where the route starts. As a general rule in Central New Jersey, the further west you go, the less traffic you'll encounter and the more rural the ride will be. However, the further west you go, the more hills you are likely to encounter.

I've changed the previous geographic organization within each section. Now routes appear in mileage order, from shortest to longest.

Route titles generally contain the origin point and an important destination along the way. All routes are loops and return to their starting points.

Mileage is only one factor in determining which route to follow, but it's an important one. If you've never cycle-toured before, it is probably best to start with a mileage under 35. Don't let these numbers intimidate you! Even beginners can tool along at 12 mph or better on flat roads. And if you have the whole day or even half a day, you won't have to hurry to finish a 35-mile ride.

Other factors to consider are listed under each ride. They are **terrain, traffic, road conditions,** and **points of interest**. Rides designated "**Hybrid**" have a significant amount of dirt roads or paths, and are best enjoyed on fat-tired bikes, either hybrids or mountain bikes.

Terrain is probably the most important element in your decision to ride a particular route. Central Jersey terrain varies tremendously, although a good part of the region is flat. There are hills when you least expect it (such as in the Atlantic Highlands, near Sandy Hook—who expects mountains near the ocean?). And there is flat terrain just when you're tired of climbing, such as returning to Princeton from Washington Crossing. Read the terrain listing carefully, but don't be afraid to challenge yourself. After a while, what once seemed difficult will become just a "gentle roll."

Traffic is an important consideration, especially when riding on a weekday. A "moderate" road may get a little busier around 5 p.m. on a Friday. *RIDE GUIDE* routes avoid the busy roads as much as possible, but in rapidly growing areas such as Princeton or Freehold, much of the ride may contain moderate traffic. If you like routes that feature more cows than cars, look for traffic descriptions of "light", "extra light", and "positively sleepy."

Road Conditions vary greatly around New Jersey, and often even within the small area covered by a bike route. Unfortunately, with all the growth and construction around the state even many back roads suffer choppy and bumpy pavement (from sewer line digs and the like), and this is noted in the write-up for each route. Dirt roads will be noted here as well. Dirt roads quite often are the most scenic and quiet, so we do not avoid them in this book, even on routes not designated as "Hybrid."

Points of Interest indicates where you might want to get off your bike, whip out your camera, notebook, or sketchpad, spread a picnic towel, jump in for a swim, fill your water bottle, check out a museum or historic site, or stop for ice cream. Sometimes there are no specific buildings to tour or shops to see and the listing under this category will be "quiet, pretty back roads." This means you are sure to encounter beautiful spots along the way for photographing or just relaxing. That's what makes cycle-touring such a great activity!

Directions to Starting Point tells you how to reach the beginning of the route by car. NJ Transit allows bicycles on some of its Northeast Corridor trains with a permit. This will allow carless cyclists to enjoy the four rides out of Princeton and Highland Park-Griggstown, which starts several miles from the New Brunswick train station.

The **cue sheets** indicate every turn and point of interest along the way. Read them one line ahead and you'll be able to spot the next turn. On the cue sheets, **Pt.-Pt.** indicates the mileage from the last turn or point of interest. **Cume**, short for cumulative, lists total mileage from the starting point. The abbreviations in the **Direction** column are:

L	Left
R	Right
S	Straight
BL	Bear Left
BR	Bear Right
SL	Sharp Left
SR	Sharp Right

In the **streets/landmarks** column, only the street you should be on is printed in **boldface**. Watch for cautions and other warnings listed in this column pertaining to steep hills, high-traffic roads, hard-to-find turns, etc. A (T) is where the road ends in another road, and you must go either right or left.

The **maps** will help you navigate the main route as well as find shortcuts back to the starting point should you need them. They are a rough indicator only, and are not necessarily drawn to scale. The cue sheet should be used for most navigation.

The maps include markings to indicate hills, dirt roads, and busy streets. It is still a good idea to include a current local street map in your bike bag along with _RIDE GUIDE_. Road configurations can change with construction of developments, and occasionally street signs disappear or are turned around.

RIDE STARTING POINTS

1. Far Hills—pages 19, 25, 29

2. Raritan/Somerville—page 35

3. Somerset—page 41

4. Clinton—pages 49, 67

5. Bloomsbury—page 55

6. Clinton Township—page 59

7. Union Township—page 63

8. Whitehouse Station—page 73

9. Flemington—page 77

10. Manalapan/Freehold—pages 85, 121

11. Highland Park—page 89

12. Allaire State Park—pages 93, 103

13. Cheesequake State Park—pages 99, 133

14. Island Beach State Park—page 109

15. Lincroft—page 115

16. Aberdeen—page 125

17. Princeton—pages 141, 147, 151, 159

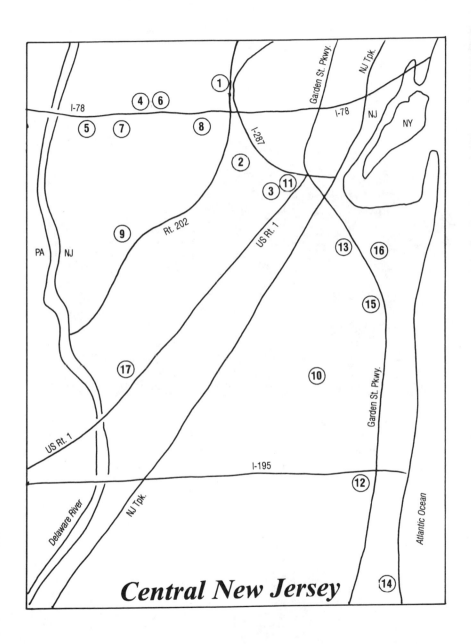

Central New Jersey

Far Hills Station is the starting point for three rides in this book. The Renaissance Revival-style structure was built by the Delaware, Lackawanna & Western Railroad in 1914, and listed on the State and National Registers of Historic Places in 1984. Of particular interest to hungry cyclists returning to their cars after an exhilarating ride is Butler's Pantry Trackside, the restaurant housed inside.

Rides Starting in Somerset County

Somerset County is an old, agricultural county in the heart of Central Jersey that has been transformed in recent decades to a pleasant mixture of agriculture, clean corporate campuses, housing developments and industry. For the cyclist, Somerset presents a variety of terrain, from the hilly Watchung Mountains in the eastern part of the county to the gently rolling terrain along the South Branch of the Raritan River. Suburbanization is taking its toll near some of the major highways, particularly routes 202, 206, and 22, but there are still plenty of fine, quiet roads to cycle.

Far Hills Dirt Road Special is a new hybrid ride that takes advantage of the fact that estate owners in horse country prefer dirt roads to keep out the riffraff. Miles of unpaved roads, some hilly, some just rolling, are available for the pleasure of fat-tired cyclists. Expect to see plenty of horses, deer, woods, and open fields. The route also features a stop at Willowwood Arboretum and a great paved downhill to the Black River Gorge near Pottersville.

The Watchung Mountains are climbed in the **Far Hills-Washington Rock** ride, but fortunately these mountains are not as tall as those in, say, Colorado or even northwest New Jersey. Expect a good workout as you head to Washington Rock, the point where colonial military leaders watched British troop movements in the Plainfield area. The scenery is pleasant and still mostly rural, despite the closeness of this area to I-78. Be sure to stop at Leonard Buck Gardens on the way back down to Far Hills.

Far Hills-Oldwick is a classic ride featuring quiet, streamside roads, lots of open farm country, several quaint towns to explore, and general stores/cafes to dine in. Bring a camera to photograph the Black River Gorge with its fast-moving cataracts. And say hello to the biggest pig you've ever seen at a farm north of Gladstone. Be prepared for a few climbs, but expect mostly rolling terrain.

Another old cycling classic is the **Somerset Rivers Ride**, rerouted away from busy roads near Route 202. Enjoy miles of riding along the various branches and tributaries of the Raritan River, and cross a number of iron bridges dating from the turn of the 20th century. Only one large hill to climb, otherwise enjoy gently undulating countryside. Cap the tour with a visit to Duke Gardens and a tour of Somerville, home of the famous Memorial Day bike race and the Bicycling Hall of Fame.

The New Flat Century is listed in this section because it starts in Somerset County. The route proceeds to tour the entire region all the way down to the Pine Barrens, passing through Middlesex, Monmouth, Ocean, and Mercer before returning to Somerset. Riding 100 miles gives you a great sense of accomplishment, and this particular 100 miles is not that difficult because it takes advantage of the flattest sections of Central Jersey. Start early, and enjoy!

Far Hills Dirt Road Special—26.0 miles
(Hybrid)

If you have an ATB or hybrid bike and want to ride long lengths along dirt roads through estate country where the roads are purposely not paved, this is the ride for you.

Terrain: Flat near the beginning but quite hilly as you ride north into Morris County and into and out of the valley of the Black River.

Traffic: Light to moderate. More horses than cars on the dirt roads.

Road Conditions: Most of the dirt roads are in very good shape, but always be aware for ruts, loose gravel, and holes, especially while going downhill. Paved roads are in good shape but can suddenly become dirt roads.

Points of Interest: Horse country. Huge open fields. Just the gates of **estates** owned by likes of Forbes, DeLorean are visible. Expect to see foxes and hounds and perhaps hot-air balloons at any time. **Willowwood Arboretum** (gardens, hiking, picnic table); **Hacklebarney Farms** (apple cider in season); **Hacklebarney State Park** (more hiking and picnic areas); **Black River Gorge**.

Who says there are no great dirt-road rides in Central New Jersey? The residents of the Far Hills-Bedminster horse country purposely left their roads unpaved to discourage auto traffic from those curious about the homes of the rich and famous. The result is an ideal hybrid bike ride. More than 14 miles of this route are unpaved.

The area is quite beautiful. You'll see lots of large open fields, horses and cattle grazing, deer leaping, forests of old trees, rivers running, and a few very large houses (the absolutely biggest mansions are invisible from the roads. All you'll see are their gatehouses).

At the 10-mile point you'll come to Willowwood Arboretum. Be sure to use the gate next to the entrance. Don't try to ride over the cattle guard or you and your bike might suffer a fate worse than the cows.

This park was once a private arboretum that was run as a plant and tree research facility by Rutgers University before becoming a part of the Morris County Park System in 1980. It contains huge, wide meadows along the half-mile entrance roads, intimate cottage and Japanese-style rock gardens and walking paths through the trees, and a convenient picnic table and rest rooms.

Next, cycle through the hilly valley of the Black River on roads variously paved and unpaved, toward Hacklebarney State Park. Pass a photogenic old mill at the bumpy bridge over the river. At the top of the hill is Hacklebarney Farms, a mecca for the auto set in the fall and a good place for a cyclist who doesn't mind yellowjackets to wolf down some scrumptious apple cider.

Now head south along gently rolling paved roads paralleling the Black River. The turn onto Black River Road is the prelude to a phenomenal two-mile-long paved downhill leading down to and along the river, through a shady gorge and along a narrow road. Fantastic!

There's a deli in tiny Pottersville if you are hungry. Half a mile past the deli, it's back to dirt roads, big estates, rolling ups and downs. A cross of busy Route 206, then more downhills take the cyclist back to Far Hills.

Directions to Starting Point: The **Far Hills railroad station** is on Route 202, 2 miles north of I-287 Exit 22B and 6 miles south of I-287 Exit 30B. During the week, those who park at the lot before 9:30 a.m. have to pay $1.

Pt.-Pt.	Cume	Turn	Street/Landmark
0.0	0.0	R	Exit Far Hills railroad station onto **Rt. 202 South**
0.7	0.7	S	Onto **Lamington Rd./Rt. 523** (Rt. 202 goes left)
0.3	1.0	S	Cross Rt. 206 at traffic light
1.2	2.2	L	**Cedar Ridge Rd.** Turn is easy to miss. **Dirt** begins
1.3	3.5	R	**River Rd. East** (T)
0.5	4.0	R	**Larger Cross Road South**
1.3	5.3	S	Cross paved Rt. 523 onto **Larger Cross Road North**
0.4	5.7	S	To continue on **Larger Cross Road** where Holland Road goes right. Cross bridge and begin to climb
1.6	7.3	R-L	At yield sign and junction of Long Lane, **make a right then an immediate left** to continue on **Larger Cross Road**

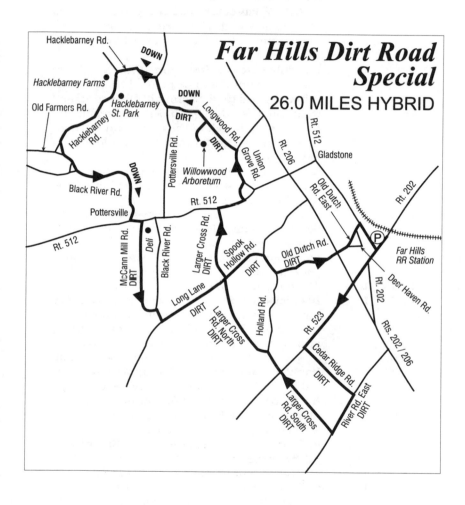

Far Hills Dirt Road Special
26.0 MILES HYBRID

Pt.-Pt.	Cume	Turn	Street/Landmark
1.3	8.6	**R**	**Rt. 512** (T) (paved)
0.3	8.9	**L**	**Union Grove Rd.**
0.5	9.4	**L**	At unmarked fork. Follow signs for Willowwood and Bamboo Brook
0.4	9.8		*CAUTION.* **Pavement suddenly ends** in midst of steep downhill. Then begin climbing. Pavement returns. Road is now called **Longwood Rd.**
0.1	9.9	**L**	Into **Willowwood Arboretum**. (*CAUTION:* There is a cattle guard across the road. Don't even think of trying to ride across it! Dismount, and walk your bike through a pedestrian gate in the fence to the left of the cattle grate.) Then ride down long gravel road through lovely meadows
0.5	10.4		Arrive at **main parking lot**. Picnic table, gardens, lovely wooded walks. Then return the way you came in
0.4	10.8	**L**	Exiting arboretum onto **Longwood Rd**. Use pedestrian gate in fence to right of cattle guard. Climb on paved road
1.1	11.9		**Pavement ends** at top of hill. Descend on hard-packed dirt
0.2	12.1	**R**	At stop sign. Follow sign for Cooper Mill
0.6	12.7	**L**	**Hacklebarney Rd.** Follow signs for Cooper Mill. Steep descents. Pavement comes and goes
0.6	13.3		Cross Black River by picturesque **old stone mill.** Very steep climb ahead on dirt road
0.3	13.6	**L**	At paved intersection (away from Cooper Mill). **Hacklebarney Farms** (cider, apples) driveway will be on the right after making the turn
0.6	14.2		**Hacklebarney State Park** entrance on left
0.7	14.9	**L**	At fork onto **Hacklebarney Rd.** Old Farmers Rd. goes right
0.5	15.4	**L**	At "Y" intersection at top of hill onto **Black River Rd.** Prepare for incredible downhill
2.6	18.0	**L**	At fork, to continue on **Black River Rd.**
0.1	18.1	**L**	At stop sign, onto **Rt. 512** (unmarked)
0.2	18.3	**R**	**McCann Mill Rd. Deli** just past the turn on Rt. 512
0.6	18.9		**Pavement suddenly disappears** into a rutted dirt road

Pt.-Pt.	Cume	Turn	Street/Landmark
0.2	19.1		**Curve left** and cross the Black River on skinny one-lane bridge. Pavement returns
0.0	19.1	R	**Black River Rd.** (T, no sign, paved)
1.2	20.3	L	**Long Lane** (unpaved)
1.7	22.0	S	At stop sign, crossing Larger Cross Road. Road changes name to **Spook Hollow Rd.**, although no sign indicates this. Primarily downhill stretch, watch your speed on loose gravel
1.5	23.5	R	**Holland Rd.** (T)
0.2	23.7	L	**Old Dutch Rd. West**
0.6	24.3		Pavement returns for good
0.3	24.6	S	Cross Rt. 206 at stop sign onto **Old Dutch Rd. East.** (*CAUTION:* Extremely busy road. Walk bikes!)
0.0	24.6	BL	At fork to continue on **Old Dutch Rd. East.** Deer Haven Rd. goes right
0.4	25.0		**Cross narrow bridge** at end of fast downhill. Watch your speed, because immediately following bridge is the next turn
0.0	25.0	R	**Rt. 512** (T) (no sign)
0.8	25.8	L	**Rt. 202** (traffic light)
0.2	26.0	L	**Far Hills railroad station**. End of route

Far Hills-Washington Rock
29.5 MILES

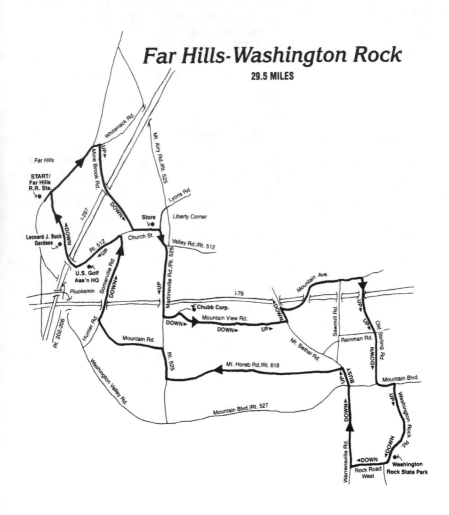

Far Hills-Washington Rock—29.5 miles

Many cyclists ride west from Far Hills, but only a few ride east—into the hills! This route is based on a foggy memory of huffing and puffing up a huge hill in the Watchung Mountains to see where Washington looked down on British troop movements—now a rather unpicturesque view of the Plainfield area. Nevertheless it is a pretty, lightly traveled, and challenging route.

Terrain: Hilly. The rises and falls are gentle but continuous to Liberty Corner, and get less gentle as you approach Washington Rock. Mt. Horeb Road and Mountain Road on the return are as close as you get to flat in this area, which means pleasantly rolling.

Traffic: Surprisingly light, considering how close you are to I-78. A little busy near Washington Rock and on Mt. Bethel Road.

Road Conditions: Good. A short stretch of dirt found on this route in the previous edition has been paved.

Points of Interest: Washington Rock State Park (overlook); **U.S. Golf Association headquarters and museum** (open seven days); **Leonard J. Buck Gardens** (a Somerset County Park); pleasant but hilly riding in the Watchung Mountains.

The I-78 corridor in central New Jersey is undergoing rapid development, but development is slower to come in the steeper terrain of Warren and Bernards Township, Somerset County. This route explores the still-quiet backroads of these communities. The destination of this route is Washington Rock State Park, a postage-stamp sized piece of green that is home to a historic overlook used by the troops of the Founding Father to monitor British troop movements.

Head up from Far Hills on Mine Brook Road. Pass some pretty horse farms coming into Liberty Corner, a quaint old hamlet that has a food store stocked with cyclist fuel.

Next, head east through Warren Township. Mountain View Road goes down for most of its length, before obeying the laws of physics and climbing steeply. As you approach Washington Rock, the hills become a little bit steeper yet, especially Old Stirling Road. So take a rest by the Rock and enjoy the view of Central Jersey—just think of what the cyclists down there in the flatlands are missing!

The return trip isn't as difficult as the outbound ride—perhaps because your quadriceps have warmed up. Mount Horeb and Mountain Roads are very gentle in terrain changes. There are some tremendous downhills as you approach Far Hills. And it's worth stopping in the midst of one such hill to view the unusual rock formations and cliff-dwelling flowers of the Leonard J. Buck Garden.

Directions to Starting Point: The **Far Hills railroad station** is on Route 202, 2 miles north of I-287 Exit 22B and 6 miles south of I-287 Exit 30B. During the week, those who park at the lot before 9:30 a.m. have to pay $1.

Pt.-Pt.	Cume	Turn	Street/Landmark
0.0	0.0	**L**	Exit Far Hills railroad station and **turn left** on **Rt. 202 North**
1.6	1.6	**R**	**Whitenack Rd.**
0.2	1.8	**R**	**Mine Brook Rd.**
2.4	4.2	**L**	**Church St.** (T)
0.4	4.6		**Store** on left
0.1	4.7	**R**	**Valley Rd./Rt. 512 East** (T)
0.3	5.0	**BR**	**Martinsville Rd./Rt. 525 South**
1.1	6.1	**L**	**Mountain View Rd.** Turn is first left past I-78 overpass (traffic light)
0.3	6.4	**BR**	To continue on **Mountain View Rd.** Entrance to Chubb Corp. is straight ahead
3.2	9.6	**L**	At unmarked T and stop sign, toward Millington and Basking Ridge
0.5	10.1	**R**	**Mountain Ave.** No street sign! Turn is near the bottom of a steep downhill, just past Cooper & Hipp Well Drilling
0.3	10.4		Cross over I-78
1.3	11.7	**R**	**Old Stirling Rd.** Turn is just before a narrow bridge
0.8	12.5	**S**	Cross Reinman Rd. (stop sign)
1.4	13.9	**L**	**Mountain Blvd.** (T)
0.5	14.4	**R**	**Washington Rock Rd.**
1.2	15.6		**Washington Rock State Park** on left (viewpoint)
0.0	15.6	**BR**	After leaving park, continue in same direction then **bear right** onto **Rock Road West**
0.9	16.5	**R**	**Warrenville Rd.** (T; no sign)
0.9	17.4	**S**	Cross Mountain Blvd./Rt. 527 at traffic light onto **Mount Bethel Rd./Rt. 651 North**

Pt.-Pt.	Cume	Turn	Street/Landmark
0.5	17.9	L	**Mt. Horeb Rd./Rt. 618**
3.6	21.5	R	**Rt. 525** (T)
0.8	22.3	L	**Mountain Rd.**
2.1	24.4	R	**Somerville Rd.** (T)
1.8	26.2	L	**Rt. 512 West** (T; no sign)
1.0	27.2		**U.S. Golf Association Headquarters and Museum** on left
1.3	28.5		**Leonard J. Buck Gardens** on left (0.1 miles down Layton Rd.)
1.0	29.5	L	**Rt. 202 South** (T)
0.0	29.5	R	**Immediate right into Far Hills railroad station.** End of route

"Lest we forget"—the plaque affixed to the rock from which George Washington monitored British troop movements in the Plainfield Valley during the spring of 1777.

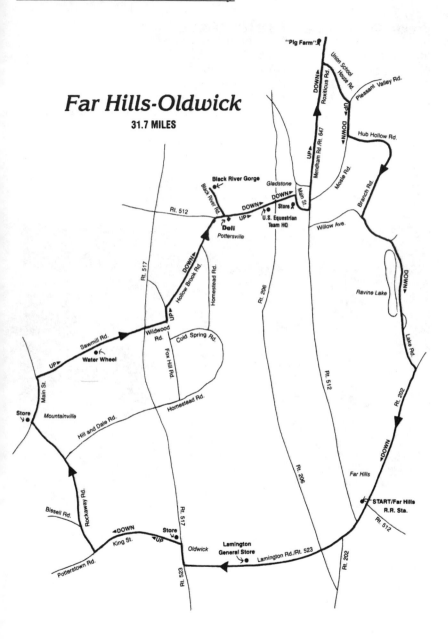

Far Hills-Oldwick
31.7 MILES

"Pig Farm"

DOWN

Union School House Rd.

Roxticus Rd.

Pleasant Valley Rd.

UP

Mendham Rd./Rt. 647

DOWN

Hub Hollow Rd.

Maple Rd.

Black River Gorge

Gladstone

DOWN

DOWN

Branch Rd.

Black River Rd.

Rt. 512

DOWN

UP

Store

Main St.

U.S. Equestrian Team HQ

Willow Ave.

Deli

Pottersville

DOWN

Hollow Brook Rd.

Homestead Rd.

Rt. 517

Ravine Lake

UP

DOWN

Rt. 206

Lake Rd.

Sawmill Rd.

Wildwood Rd.

Cold Spring Rd.

Rt. 202

Water Wheel

Fox Hill Rd.

UP

Main St.

Store

Mountainville

Homestead Rd.

Hill and Dale Rd.

Rt. 512

DOWN

Far Hills

Rockaway Rd.

Bissell Rd.

Rt. 517

Store

START/Far Hills R.R. Sta.

DOWN

King St.

UP

Oldwick

Rt. 512

Potterstown Rd.

Rt. 523

Lamington General Store

Lamington Rd./Rt. 523

Rt. 206

Rt. 202

Far Hills-Oldwick—31.7 miles

This classic route has appeared in RIDE GUIDEs *since they were first published in 1985. Because so many cyclists consider this their favorite ride, it is repeated here.*

Terrain: Rolling to hilly, with a few long climbs and descents.

Traffic: Light between Oldwick and Pottersville, and again between Gladstone and Far Hills. Otherwise, moderate.

Road Conditions: Smooth, for the most part, but some choppy shoulders, especially on Pottersville and Roxiticus Roads.

Points of Interest: "General Store" (antiques and folk art) in Lamington; real old-time **general stores** with tables for eating in Oldwick and Mountainville; **Black River Gorge**; **U.S. Equestrian Team headquarters** (occasional competitions); beautiful scenery including streams, horse farms, and **Ravine Lake**.

What makes a route a classic, one that cyclists ride again and again? Ride from the Far Hills train station into the horse-and-antique country near Oldwick and Mountainville and find out.

The terrain starts out gently rolling on Lamington Road, a straight six-mile stretch to Oldwick. Antique and art buffs might enjoy the Lamington General Store, on the right in the midst of the small hamlet of Lamington, which is surrounded by cornfields and woods.

Oldwick is a settlement of more substantial size, with a row of old buildings, shops and a photogenic church. The general store has been a favorite of cyclists for years—be sure to sample some of the home-baked goodies.

The section of the route from Oldwick to Pottersville is what most people remember about this classic. Riding down tree-shaded Rockaway Road, gently climbing next to the babbling brook, huge horse farms on the right—this puts you in a relaxed state of mind. If you haven't snacked at Oldwick, the little store in Mountainville will feed you well. Sit at one of the two tables on the porch sipping homemade iced tea and you will almost feel like you're in a small European country village.

Sawmill Road is a climb, but have your cameras ready for a huge water wheel on the right. The home next to it is called, appropriately enough, Water Wheel in the Woods.

Wildwood Road, the flatter extension of Sawmill, has stone houses surrounded by stone walls, and evokes a 19th-century atmosphere. Then get ready for some downhill action as you approach Hollow Brook Road. It's a free ride for two miles into Pottersville.

The Black River Gorge is a great lunch spot (mind the private property signs, however. There is a section past several houses and a dam that is state-owned). Exiting Pottersville, you are out of the woods and back into open pastureland. A climb followed by a descent takes you by Hamilton Farm, home of the U.S. Equestrian Team. Further descent brings you into the borough of Gladstone, which is characterized by the exotic car dealership in town that specializes in Bentleys and Jaguars.

Roxiticus Road is an uphill battle into Mendham Township. At the bottom of the following downhill is an amazing farm with a menagerie of animals featuring donkeys, horses, sheep, and an enormous sow who has a big crop of cute piglets every spring.

The final treat of this route is a ride by Ravine Lake, a narrow body of water surrounded by high hills (none of which you have to ride over). When you return to Far Hills, you might wish to enjoy a fine dinner at Butler's Pantry, the restaurant in the train station (closed Sunday). This is a fitting end to a day of cycling in the finest of Somerset and Hunterdon horse country.

Directions to Starting Point: The **Far Hills railroad station** is on Route 202, 2 miles north of I-287 Exit 22B and 6 miles south of I-287 Exit 30B. During the week, those who park at the lot before 9:30 a.m. have to pay $1.

Pt.-Pt.	Cume	Turn	Street/Landmark
0.0	0.0	**R**	Exit Far Hills railroad station onto **Rt. 202 South**
0.7	0.7	**S**	Onto **Lamington Rd./Rt. 523** (Rt. 202 goes left)
0.3	1.0	**S**	Cross Rt. 206 at traffic light
3.9	4.9		**Lamington General Store** (antiques) on right
1.7	6.6	**R**	**Oldwick Rd./Rt. 517** (T)

Pt.-Pt.	Cume	Turn	Street/Landmark
0.5	7.1	L	**King St. Oldwick General Store** on this corner. Road will change name eventually to **Potterstown Rd.**
1.6	8.7	R	**Rockaway Rd.** (stop sign)
0.2	8.9	BR	To continue on **Rockaway Rd.** Bissell Rd. goes left
2.6	11.5	R	**Main St.** (T), in the center of the hamlet of Mountainville. **Chelsea Kitchen General Store** straight ahead of you at this intersection
0.2	11.7	BR	**Sawmill Rd.**, at fork
0.9	12.6		Look for water wheel in the woods on right
1.2	13.8	S	Cross Rt. 517 (unmarked) at stop sign. Road changes name to **Wildwood Rd.**
0.6	14.4	L	**Fox Hill Rd.** (T)
0.2	14.6	R	**Hollow Brook Rd.** (stop sign). (*CAUTION:* Control your speed on the upcoming steep, winding, bumpy downhill)
2.2	16.8	R	**Fairmount Rd. East/Rt. 512** (T)
0.3	17.1	SL	**Black River Rd.** Turn is a hard-to-spot narrow sharp left in the midst of a steep downhill curve. Look for a pretty white house with black shutters
0.3	17.4		Picnic alongside the Black River (mind the Posted signs). Then return the way you pedaled in
0.3	17.7	L	**Rt. 512. Deli** on right after the turn.
0.3	18.0	L	Curve left to continue on **Rt. 512/Pottersville Rd.** (no signs). Large church is on your right and small bank is on your left
2.1	20.1		**U.S. Equestrian Team Headquarters** on right
0.4	20.5	S	Cross Rt. 206 at traffic light
0.6	21.1	R	**Main St.** (T) (toward Far Hills/Bedminster). **Deli** on right at corner
0.3	21.4	L	**Mendham Rd./Rt. 647 North** (T). Becomes **Roxiticus Rd.**
3.5	24.9		At bottom of hill, check out interesting farm with huge pig and other assorted animals. Then reverse direction and pedal a short way back up hill
0.2	25.1	L	**Union School House Rd.**
0.7	25.8	R	**Mosle Rd.**, at fork

Pt.-Pt.	Cume	Turn	Street/Landmark
0.6	26.4	L	**Hub Hollow Rd.** (just before stone-walled narrow bridge)
1.5	27.9	L	**Willow Ave.** (T)
0.5	28.4	R	**Lake Rd.** (no signs). Turn is a fork just past a bridge. You will ride next to **Ravine Lake** shortly after this turn
2.5	30.9	R	**Rt. 202** (T; no signs)
0.8	31.7	R	Into **Far Hills railroad station**. End of route

For upscale dining, the Tewksbury Inn in Oldwick. In the background is the Oldwick General Store, one of the most popular hangouts for cyclists in Central Jersey.

The Neshanic flea market is on the left after you cross yet another old iron bridge over the South Branch. Even if the flea market isn't operating (it usually is on weekends in late spring, summer, and fall), you might wish to stop by the bridge and take photographs.

Circle around the estate of the Duke family, one of the richest in New Jersey. If you are riding here between noon and 4 p.m. in the cooler weather months, you can enter Duke Gardens. The world-famous gardens contain 11 different horticultural settings under an acre of glass. Note that the gardens are closed in the summer when the heat under the glass is uncomfortable for visitors.

Next, cycle along a bike path that allows you to avoid busy Finderne Avenue in Manville. Ride through Somerville—an important town for cycling—on quiet side streets. The annual Tour of Somerville race takes place on Memorial Day. On Mountain Avenue, look for a bicycle enclosed in glass and concrete. This is the actual bicycle used by Furman Frederick Kugler to win the first two Somerville races in 1940 and 1941. Note the leather toe straps and wooden rims!

Two blocks away at 166 West Main Street is the Bicycling Hall of Fame. This interesting shrine to racing, especially bike racing in New Jersey and New York City in the first half of the 20th century, is open weekdays from noon to 3 p.m. or by appointment; call (908) 722-3620.

A short run through Raritan and along the river of the same name brings you back to Duke Island Park. During the summer, top off your ride with a band concert held weekly at the band shell in the park—check the park bulletin board for the schedule.

Directions to Starting Point: Duke Island Park is off Old York Road (Route 567), west of Somerville and Raritan. From I-287 Southbound, use Exit 17 to Route 202/206 South. From I-287 Northbound, Exit 14 (Route 22 West) will take you to Route 202/206 South. Follow Route 206 about 0.5 miles south of the Somerville Circle (where it leaves Route 202) to the first traffic light (just past railroad underpass), which is Somerset Street. Turn right, then proceed 2.3 miles to the park (on left). The ride begins in Parking Lot A, which is to the left (turn after crossing the little bridge on the park entrance road).

Pt.-Pt.	Cume	Turn	Street/Landmark
0.0	0.0		From **Parking Lot A**, turn right and right again to exit Duke Island Park
0.2	0.2	**L**	**Rt. 567/Old York Rd.** (T)
1.8	2.0	**L**	To continue on **Route 567**. Route 637 goes straight
0.4	2.4	**L**	**Rt. 567 South/South Branch Rd.** (T)
3.7	6.1	**R**	**Rt. 629 North** (T)
1.7	7.8	**L**	**Old York Rd.** (turn comes up suddenly in midst of small historic settlement)
2.6	10.4	**BL**	At stop sign at end of Old York Rd. onto unmarked road
0.7	11.1	**L**	**Hillsborough Rd.** Changes name to **Three Bridges Rd.**
1.0	12.1	**L**	**Higginsville Rd.**
0.1	12.2		Rest stop by river at far end of bridge. Then cycle back the way you came in
0.1	12.3	**L**	**Three Bridges Rd.** (T)
0.4	12.7	**L**	At fork to continue on **Three Bridges Rd.**, which goes along river. Hockenbury Rd. goes right
1.2	13.9	**L**	**Woodfern Rd.** (T) (cross river immediately)
0.8	14.7	**R**	At T to continue on **Woodfern Rd.** Lehigh Rd. goes left
1.0	15.7	**R**	**Blackpoint Rd.** (stop sign)
1.2	16.9	**S**	Cross Amwell Rd. at stop sign onto **Montgomery Rd.**
1.1	18.0	**L**	**Wertsville Rd.**
0.8	18.8	**R**	**Long Hill Rd.** (T)
1.2	20.0	**L**	**Zion Rd.**
2.6	22.6	**R**	**Amwell Rd.** (T)
0.1	22.7	**L**	**Rt. 567 North**
0.9	23.6	**L**	Cross old iron bridge into Neshanic Station. Turn is at bottom of hill
0.1	23.7		**Flea market** on left
0.1	23.8	**R**	**Pearl St.** Becomes **Olive St.**
0.2	24.0		**Store** on right
0.1	24.1	**R**	**Pleasant Run Rd./Rt. 667 North** (T; go under railroad underpass immediately)
0.4	24.5	**R**	**Rt. 567 South** (toward South Branch/ Neshanic)
0.5	25.0	**L**	Onto unmarked **River Rd.** toward South Branch. Turn is in midst of red clay embankments

Pt.-Pt.	Cume	Turn	Street/Landmark
2.4	27.4	**S**	At stop sign to continue on **River Rd./Rt. 625 North**
0.6	28.0	**S**	Continue straight on **River Rd./Rt. 625 North.** Rt. 606 West goes left. *OPTION:* Turn **left** here for shortcut cutting 12 miles off route. Then turn **right** at **Rt. 567** and follow it back to Duke Island Park (see map)
3.2	31.2	**SR**	**Roycefield Rd.** (no sign). The fenced-in **Duke Estate** is on your left as you turn. *OPTION:* To cut eight miles off the route total, go **straight** here to eventually join with **Canal St.** between miles 38.4 and 38.8 of the cue sheet (see map)
1.0	32.2	**L**	**Dukes Pkwy. West** (stop sign)
1.5	33.7	**L**	**Rt. 206 North** (T; traffic light) *CAUTION:* Very busy road. A shoulder will appear shortly
0.4	34.1	**R**	**Dukes Pkwy.** (next traffic light). To visit **Duke Gardens**, turn **left** at this intersection (do so by going right, U-turning and waiting for green light on Dukes Pkwy.). Entrance to garden (open noon to 4 p.m. daily except in summer) is in a few hundred feet
1.7	35.8	**L**	Onto **bike path**, just before intersection of Finderne Ave.
0.2	36.0		Bike path from here on consists of a sidewalk (well-paved) going against traffic on Finderne Ave., crossing Raritan River
0.6	36.6	**L**	**Bridgewater Ave.**
0.5	37.1	**R**	**Adamsville Rd.** (T)
0.1	37.2	**S**	Cross Main St. at stop sign
0.1	37.3	**L**	**Adams St.**
0.3	37.6	**L**	**Post St.** (T)
0.1	37.7	**R**	Curve right onto **Grant Ave.**
0.2	37.9	**R**	**Vanderveer Ave.** (T)
0.1	38.0	**L**	**E. High St.** (stop sign)
1.1	39.1	**L**	**Mountain Ave.** (T)
0.1	39.2	**S**	Cross West End Ave. Note **Furman Frederick Kugler's bicycle** in glass and concrete on right after intersection. If you wish to visit the **Bicycling Hall of Fame**, make a **left** here and cycle two blocks to 166 West Main Street (the Hall is located in a small office building behind a brokerage office)

Pt.-Pt.	Cume	Turn	Street/Landmark
0.1	37.8	**R**	**Somerset St.** (traffic light)
0.2	38.0	**S**	Cross Rt. 206 at traffic light
0.3	38.3	**L**	**Thompson St.** (traffic light)
0.1	38.4	**R**	Curve right onto **Canal St.** Use sidewalk to circumvent metal barrier to continue on Canal St.
0.4	38.8	**L**	**Rt. 567** (T; no signs)
1.6	40.4	**L**	Into **Duke Island Park**
0.2	40.6	**L**	Into **Parking Lot A**. End of route

Memorial to Furman Frederick Kugler on Mountain Avenue in Somerville. This is the actual bicycle Kugler used win the first two Somerville bicycle races in 1940 and 1941, right down to the wooden rims and leather toe straps. Kugler was killed in World War II, but the race is still held every Memorial Day weekend.

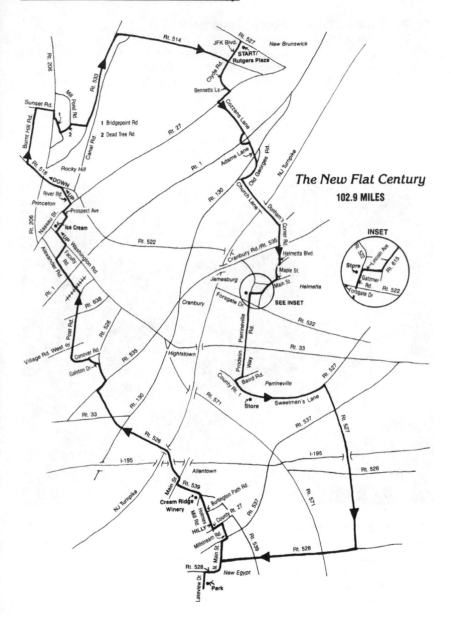

The New Flat Century

102.9 MILES

The New Flat Century—102.9 miles

This ride is still an ideal first century for anyone looking for a challenge, and can be done by anyone who's mastered a 55-mile ride because it's flat!

Terrain: Mostly flat. A few roads have some rollers, and only a very occasional short, steep hill, which are noted on the cue sheet.

Traffic: Light, except near the towns. For the most part, you ride on rural or suburban back roads. Numbered highways are somewhat busier.

Road Conditions: Very good. Smooth and easy cycling; no dirt roads.

Points of Interest: Old homes and shops in **Allentown**; **Cream Ridge Winery**; **Princeton (University** and shops; ice cream!); the thrill of accomplishment.

M e, ride 100 miles? Yes, you! If you have ridden many of the hilly rides in this book, not only can you do this century, but you should! It's one of the flattest, prettiest, and most traffic-free centuries you'll find.

Start by 7 a.m. if you intend to finish the ride—rushing to beat a setting sun is no fun after 80 miles. Even with stops, you should be back to your car by 5 p.m., and possibly earlier. Bring plenty of water and munchies. Have room in your bike bag for clothing you will shed as the early morning chill disappears.

You will pedal out of suburban New Brunswick and through the developing sprawl of the Route 1 corridor before reaching the relative tranquility (scenery-wise) of the woodsy and agricultural areas south of Jamesburg. Mile after mile goes by as you aim for the Pine Barrens, all easy, flat miles with few turns to worry about and an occasional store should you need food or water.

Lunch is at the 50-mile mark in New Egypt. Eat in a park by a river, or try one of the many delis or luncheonettes in this small town. Don't be surprised if you see huge military aircraft overhead—McGuire Air Force Base is close by.

The return route takes you through Allentown, a very pretty town of shops and old homes. The old mill on the left is worth a stop and a quick look around. Then, at 75 miles, comes the welcome Princeton ice cream stop. Line up with students and faculty for yummy confections.

Return to your car by way of the Millstone Valley. It will feel good to get off your bike. Congratulations—you've completed 100 miles!

Directions to Starting Point: Rutgers Plaza is on Easton Avenue (Route 527) in the Somerset section of Franklin Township, outside of New Brunswick. Take I-287 to Exit 11 (Route 527 South). The shopping center is on the right, about 2.5 miles south of the highway exit.

Pt.-Pt.	Cume	Turn	Street/Landmark
0.0	0.0	L	Exit Rutgers Plaza near Burger King by turning left onto **JFK Blvd.**
2.0	2.0	S	Cross Hamilton St. at traffic light. Road becomes **Clyde Rd.** Road changes name again eventually to **Bennetts Lane**
2.1	4.1	R	**Rt. 27** (T) (traffic light). *CAUTION*—busy road
0.9	5.0	L	**Cozzens Lane** (first traffic light)
1.1	6.1	R	Toward Rt. 1 North and Adams Station
0.1	6.2	S	Cross Rt. 1 at light; follow Adams Station signs. You will be on **Adams Lane**
1.2	7.4	S	Cross Rt. 130 at traffic light
0.1	7.5	R	**Old Georges Rd.** (T)
0.6	8.1	L	**Church Lane** (church on left by corner)
2.8	10.9	R	At fork (T) onto **Dunham's Corner Rd.** (no sign; turn occurs just past overpass over N.J. Turnpike)
1.5	12.4	S	Cross Cranbury Road at traffic light. Road becomes **Helmetta Blvd.**
1.0	13.4	R	**Maple St.** (T)
0.5	13.9	R	**Main St.** (T)
0.8	14.7	BL	**Rt. 615 South** (fork). Gulf station on corner will be on your right if you chose the correct fork
0.8	15.5	R	**Lincoln Ave.** (continuing on **Rt. 615 South**)
0.4	15.9	BL	Cross railroad (Junction Rt. 522) then left onto **Gatzmer Ave.** Cumberland Farms (**food**) on right

Pt.-Pt.	Cume	Turn	Street/Landmark
0.6	16.5	S	At stop sign. Cross Forsgate Dr. onto **Perrineville Rd.**
6.1	22.6	S	Cross Rt. 33 at traffic light. Road becomes **Prodelin Way**
2.2	24.8	R	**Baird Rd.** (T)
0.0	24.8	L	Immediate left onto **Monmouth County Rt. 1** (T) (no sign)
1.3	26.1		Roy's Deli on right (**food**). Road has changed name to **Sweetman's Lane**
3.6	29.7	R	**Rt. 527 South**
2.0	31.7	S	At traffic light to continue on **Rt. 527 South** (cross Rt. 537)
4.0	35.7	S	Cross over I-195
0.5	36.2	S	Cross Rt. 526 (traffic light)
2.6	38.8	R	**Rt. 528 West** (traffic light)
2.6	41.4	S	Cross Rt. 571 (traffic light)
5.3	46.7	S	Cross Rt. 539 (traffic light)
2.8	49.5	L	At stop sign to continue on **Rt. 528 West**. Entering **New Egypt**. Delis, stores, and restaurants available
0.2	49.7	L	**Lakeview Drive**
0.1	49.8		Park on left by a river (lunch stop). Then U-turn and ride back to Rt. 528
0.1	49.9	R	**Rt. 528 East** (returning the way you came in)
0.4	50.3	S	At blinker light onto **North Main Street** (Rt. 528 goes right). A school will be on your left. Road changes name to **High Bridge Rd.**
1.9	52.2	R	**Rt. 537** (T) (*CAUTION*—busy road)
0.1	52.3	L	**Millstream Road**
0.6	52.9	L	**County Rt. 27** (T) (stop sign; no street sign)
0.4	53.3	R	**Holmes Mill Rd.** (first stop sign; no street sign) (*Note*: you will encounter some hills here)
2.0	55.3	S	To continue on **Holmes Mill Rd.** (Burlington Path Road goes right)
1.6	56.9	BL	**Rt. 539** (T) (stop sign; no street sign). Rt. 539 is the main road—do not turn onto other small road coming in at sharp angle. **Cream Ridge Winery** will be on your left after the turn
2.9	59.8	R	**South Main St.**, Allentown (T)
0.4	60.2	L	**Rt. 526 West (Church St.)** (*CAUTION*—busy road)

Pt.-Pt.	Cume	Turn	Street/Landmark
1.2	61.4	**S**	Cross I-195
0.4	61.8	**S**	Cross N.J. Turnpike
1.9	63.7	**S**	Cross Rt. 130 (traffic light)
0.3	64.0	**BL/R**	Bear left at traffic light to cross Rt. 33 then make an immediate right to continue on **Rt. 526 West**
3.0	67.0	**R**	At stop sign (junction Rt. 535) to continue on **Rt. 526 West**
0.3	67.3	**L**	At traffic light to continue on **Rt. 526 West**
0.6	67.9	**L**	**Galston Dr.** (after bridge)
0.5	68.4	**L**	**Conover Rd.** (T)
1.2	69.6	**R**	**South Post Rd.** (T)
0.5	70.1	**S**	Cross Village Rd. West
1.5	71.6	**S**	Cross Clarksville Rd. (Rt. 638) (traffic light)
0.7	72.3	**L**	**Alexander Rd.** (street sign on right; cross railroad immediately)
1.4	73.7	**S**	Cross Rt. 1 (traffic light)
1.1	74.8	**R**	**Faculty Rd.** (traffic light)
0.5	75.3	**L**	**Washington Rd.** (traffic light)
0.8	76.1	**R**	**Nassau St.** (T) (Thomas Sweet's **ice cream** on right in one block). After break, walk bikes on Nassau St. sidewalk back to **Washington Rd.** and turn **left**
0.2	76.3	**R**	**Prospect Ave.** (traffic light)
2.1	78.4	**R**	**Princeton-Kingston Rd. (Rt. 27)** (third stop sign after first traffic light)
0.7	79.1	**L**	**River Rd. (Rt. 605)** (first traffic light). You will encounter hills here. Road becomes **Crescent Ave.** in Rocky Hill
2.5	81.6	**L**	**Rt. 518 West** (T)
0.4	82.0	**S**	Cross Rt. 206 (traffic light)
2.1	84.1	**R**	**Burnt Hill Rd.**
0.5	84.6	**R**	Road curves right after one-lane bridge
1.6	86.2	**R**	**Sunset Rd.** (T)
0.8	87.0	**R**	**Van Horne Rd. (Rt. 206)** (T)
0.1	87.1	**L**	**Bridgepoint Rd.**
0.8	87.9	**L**	**Dead Tree Rd.**
0.3	88.2	**BR**	At fork past mill pond to continue on **Dead Tree Rd.** (Mill Pond Rd. goes left)
1.0	89.2	**L**	**River Rd./Rt. 533 North** (T)
7.0	96.2	**R**	**Rt. 514 East** (traffic light)
2.7	98.9	**BR**	At traffic light to continue on **Rt. 514 East**

2.0	100.9	**L**	**JFK Blvd.** (traffic light)
2.0	102.9	**R**	Into **Rutgers Plaza.** End of route

Water wheel and millrace on the mill in Clinton, Hunterdon County

Rides Starting In Hunterdon County

Hilly is the operative word for Hunterdon County. Some of the routes in this county are among the hilliest in *RIDE GUIDE*, but several of the routes contain only gently rolling terrain, or just a few steep climbs. For scenery, Hunterdon is hard to top, since hills reward cyclists with tremendous panoramic views. The county is still fairly lightly developed and heavily agricultural, so count on lots of quiet back roads.

Hunterdon's two large reservoirs (Spruce Run and Round Valley) both have public beaches. Solberg Airport in Readington Township hosts the second-largest balloon festival in the United States in July, and there is always much to see and explore in the towns along the Delaware River, which forms the county's western boundary.

Clinton-Pittstown is a new hybrid ride featuring pretty countryside south of Clinton. Pedal by horse farms adjacent to the South Branch of the Raritan River. Then head west to Pittstown through classic Central Jersey open-field countryside on rolling roads. The return to Clinton is through intimate "hollows" and stream valleys on quiet, narrow roads.

Bloomsbury-Riegelsville, the shortest road tour in *RIDE GUIDE/Central Jersey*, starts with a long uphill that is the only climb of the route. Beautiful, quiet roads wind downhill from the summit to the Delaware River, passing pretty stream gorges cloaked in hemlock woods. Along the Delaware, explore the river towns of Milford and Riegelsville and refresh yourself with wild raspberries that grow in profusion in summer.

Tewksbury-Hacklebarney heads north out of Hunterdon into Morris County. The destination is Hacklebarney State Park with its pretty river gorge, a popular cider mill, and a restored grist mill. Also for your enjoyment are several old-fashioned general stores. Expect a number of challenging climbs on this tour.

Northern Hunterdon Hillbilly is for cyclists who hate flat roads. The reward for climbing all these ridges is great views of the Musconetcong Valley—and a swim at Spruce Run. Very ambitious cyclists can combine this route with the "South Brancher" for a 53.7-mile tour.

Need peace and tranquility? **South Brancher** fills the bill by following the scenic South Branch of the Raritan River for 11 flat miles. Fly-fishermen and numerous birds will be your only company much of the way. The return crosses a few ridges and passes Wood Glen General Store on the way to a swim stop at Spruce Run Reservoir.

Round the Valley circles Round Valley Reservoir. Enjoy tremendous views from the tops of ridges. The climbs are not too difficult, except for one big uphill near the reservoir. Return via the photogenic old villages of Lebanon and Whitehouse.

Flemington-Raven Rock also heads west for the Delaware River. This route features Bull's Island, a state park that anchors a pedestrian bridge to Lumberville, Pa. An alternative to riding on quiet Route 29 along the river is pedaling on the even quieter and very smooth Delaware & Raritan Canal path. Bring your cameras to photograph New Jersey's only covered bridge, and bring your appetite for the delectables available at Bridge Cafe, a pretty outdoor riverside eatery in Frenchtown.

Clinton-Pittstown—24.2 miles
(Hybrid)

Definitely the prettiest of the new "hybrid" (some dirt, some paved) rides in the second edition of RIDE GUIDE Central Jersey, *this route is perfect for hybrid bikes.*

Terrain: Rolling to quite hilly.

Traffic: Very light, except light to moderate on the numbered highways near Quakerstown and Pittstown.

Road Conditions: Excellent, for the most part. Even the dirt roads are fairly good.

Points of Interest: Huge horse farms; river valleys and hollows; riding along South Branch of Raritan and several other creeks.

This new route explores the farm areas south and southwest of Clinton in Hunterdon County. It includes River Road, one of the most spectacularly beautiful roads in Central Jersey with its horse farms and no new housing developments.

The ride is a contrast of shaded river and creek valleys and classic Central Jersey open-field views with rolling terrain. It passes some pretty hamlets, including Quakertown and Cherryville, as well as the slightly larger Pittstown near the end of the route, which has the only food available.

Start by heading south out of Clinton. Soon you are on a road that crosses the South Branch of the Raritan River and hugs its shore. Explore a closed section of road popular with fishermen because it heads right to the river where another bridge used to cross it.

Go up and down some paved and dirt roads to get back onto River Road. Soon you will be passing the horse farms mentioned above. Be sure to bring your camera.

After some rolling, woodsy hills and a busy crossing of Route 31, you are back on the dirt, passing more horse farms and even a racing track.

The route then heads northwest, through the shady glen of Cherryville Hollow Road, before emerging to open fields on the trek from Cherryville to Quakertown to Pittstown.

Return is via more stream valleys and wooded, rolling hills on narrow, lightly traveled roads.

The route takes you through Clinton, a quaint town with interesting stores and museums, before returning to the starting point.

Directions to Starting Point: The ride starts at the **Clinton A&P.** From Route 78 West, use Exit 15. Turn right on Route 173 and proceed 0.7 miles. The A&P will be on your left.

Pt.-Pt.	Cume	Turn	Street/Landmark
0.0	0.0		Exit A&P and turn right on **Rt. 173**
0.3	0.3	L	**Leigh St.** (traffic light). Go under I-78. Road will eventually change name to **Hamden Rd.**
1.6	1.9	R	**Hamden Rd.** Sign says Bridge Weight Limit 6 Tons 2/10 Mile Ahead
0.5	2.4	S	Where Lower Landsdown Rd. goes right, continue straight to explore the closed road heading toward the South Branch. Closed road ends at site of former bridge. Return the way you came.
0.8	3.2	L	**Lower Landsdown Rd.**
0.4	3.6	L	**Landsdown Rd.** Watch for numerous bumpy railroad crossings
0.1	3.7	L	**Sidney School Rd.**
1.2	4.9	L	**Pine Hill Rd.** Down hill
0.1	5.0		Road becomes **dirt**
0.2	5.2		**Paved** again. Steep downhill, one-lane road
0.2	5.4		**Dirt** again at bottom of steep hill
0.2	5.6		Cross one-lane bridge over the river. Pass YMCA Camp Carr
0.2	5.8	R	**Dirt** road, at T (unmarked Hamden Rd.)
0.4	6.2		Cross river. **Pavement** will return.
0.2	6.4	R	**Old Clinton Rd.** (T)
0.1	6.5	L	Past one-lane bridge, to continue on **Old Clinton Rd.** Cherryville-Stanton Rd. goes right
1.1	7.6	L	At stop sign, to continue on **Old Clinton Rd.** William Barnes Rd. goes straight
0.3	7.9	L	**River Rd.**

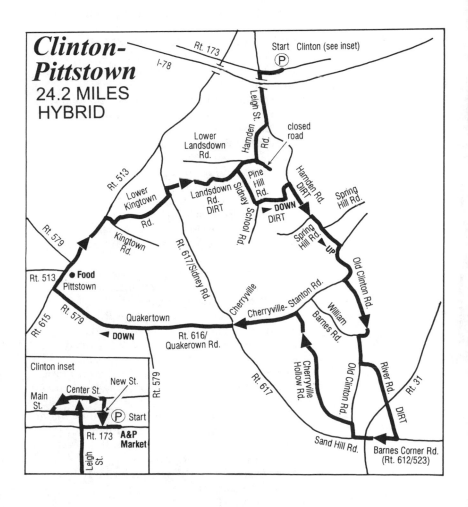

Clinton-Pittstown

24.2 MILES
HYBRID

Rt. 173

I-78

Start Clinton (see inset)
(P)

Leigh St.

Hamden St. Rd.

closed road

Lower Landsdown Rd.

Pine Hill Rd.

Hamden Rd. DIRT

Spring Hill Rd.

Rt. 513

Lower Kingtown

Landsdown Rd. DIRT

Sidney School Rd.

DOWN DIRT

Spring Hill Rd.

UP

Rt. 579

Kingtown Rd.

Rd.

Rt. 617/Sidney Rd.

Old Clinton Rd.

Rt. 513 ● Food
Pittstown

Rt. 579

Cherryville

Cherryville-Stanton Rd.

William

Barnes Rd.

Rt. 615

Quakertown

DOWN

Rt. 616/Quakerown Rd.

Cherryville Hollow Rd.

Old Clinton Rd.

River Rd.

Rt. 31

Rt. 617

DIRT

Clinton inset

New St.

Rt. 579

Main St.

Center St.

(P) Start

Rt. 173 **A&P Market**

Leigh St.

Sand Hill Rd.

Barnes Corner Rd.
(Rt. 612/523)

Pt.-Pt.	Cume	Turn	Street/Landmark
0.9	8.8	**S**	Cross Rt. 31. *DANGER*: Incredibly busy road. Walk bikes across. Be patient. There will be openings in the traffic.
0.2	9.0		Back to **dirt**—and horse farms. Racing track on left, beautiful old yellow inn-like home on right
0.8	9.8	**R**	**Bartles Corner Rd./Rt. 612/523** (T). *CAUTION*: busy road.
0.7	10.5	**S**	Cross Rt. 31 at traffic light onto **Sand Hill Rd.**
0.3	10.8	**R**	**Old Clinton Rd.**
0.2	11.0	**L**	**Cherryville Hollow Rd.** Gentle climb following a curving stream. Deep shade, wild raspberries
2.4	13.4	**L**	**Cherryville Stanton Rd.** (T)
0.4	13.8	**S**	Cross Rt. 617 at stop sign in settlement of Cherryville onto **Rt. 616/Quakertown Rd.** Sign points to Quakertown.
2.1	15.9	**S**	At junction of Rt. 579 onto **Rt. 579 North**, through Quakertown. Awesome downhill
1.3	17.2	**R**	At T, to continue on **Rt. 579 North**. Rt. 615 goes left. *CAUTION*: busy, curvy road, mostly downhill, little shoulder
0.3	17.5	**S**	**Rt. 513/579 North**. Pizza/ice cream available in **Pittstown** on right before intersection
0.1	17.6	**S**	**Rt. 513 North**. Rt. 579 goes off to left
1.0	18.6	**R**	At bottom of hill, onto **Kingtown Rd.** Red barn on corner. Cross one-lane 6-ton bridge
0.1	18.7	**L**	At fork onto **Lower Kingtown Rd.** Curvy, narrow one-lane road, mostly downhill. River valley road, deep shade combined with horse country, very pretty. Nicely paved, numerous bridges
1.2	19.9	**L-R**	At stop sign, turn left on **Sidney Rd.** then make an immediate right onto **Landsdown Rd.** (**Dirt road** but smooth). Mostly uphill
0.8	20.7		Cross bumpy railroad crossing
0.1	20.8	**R**	**Lower Landsdown Rd.** (watch for more bumpy railroad crossings)
0.3	21.1	**L**	**Hamden Rd.** (T)
0.6	21.7	**L**	At stop sign to continue on **Hamden Rd.** This will become **Leigh St.** in Clinton
1.5	23.2	**S**	Cross Rt. 173 at traffic light

Pt.-Pt.	Cume	Turn	Street/Landmark
0.1	23.3	L	**Center St.**
0.1	23.4	L	**Main St. Hunterdon Art Center** is the stone building on the right by the river. You might wish to walk your bikes on the sidewalk of the bridge (right turn) to go to **Clinton Historical Museum Village** across the river before returning to Main St. **Clinton Country Store and Eatery** (outdoor riverside ice cream cafe) is on Main Street directly across from this intersection
0.1	23.5	L	**Leigh St.** (stop sign)
0.1	23.6	R	**Center St.** Pretty houses on this street
0.2	23.8	R	**New St.**
0.1	23.9	L	**Rt. 173** (T)
0.3	24.2	L	Into **A&P parking lot.** End of route

The Hunterdon Art Center in Clinton

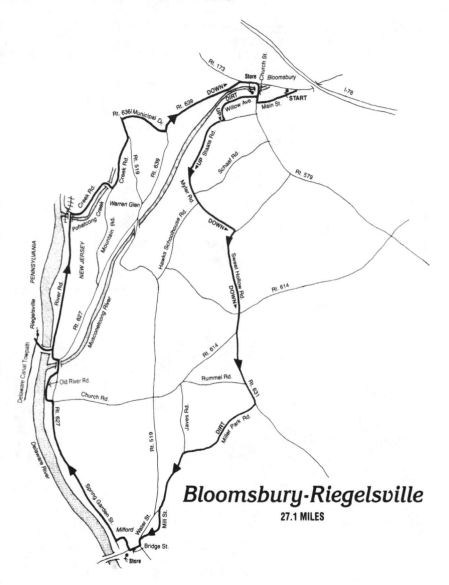

Bloomsbury-Riegelsville

27.1 MILES

Bloomsbury-Riegelsville—27.1 miles

RIDE GUIDE *books cover most of the New Jersey side of the Delaware River from the Port Jervis, N.Y. area all the way to Trenton. This is the northernmost stretch of river in the Central Jersey book, and it is a beautiful stretch!*

Terrain: A long climb at the onset, followed by seven glorious downhill miles, then flat to gently rolling back to Bloomsbury.

Traffic: Light to nonexistent.

Road Conditions: A couple of sizeable sections of dirt road, otherwise smoothly paved.

Points of Interest: Interesting river towns of **Milford, N.J.**, and **Riegelsville, Pa.**; fabulous scenery on quiet country roads.

Long ago, Bloomsbury was the site of a popular hot-air balloon festival. While the skies no longer fill with balloons once a year here (there is another festival at Solberg Airport, on the "Round The Valley" route, page 73), this small western New Jersey town is worth driving out to for fantastic cycling along the Delaware River.

Start by climbing a two-mile hill out of town. This may sound ominous, but there are no more major climbs and very few minor climbs for the rest of the ride. The reward for the two-mile climb is seven miles of downhill cruising to the Delaware.

While gravity is doing the work, you will pass several pretty stream ravines. Miller Park Road is a hard-packed dirt road that goes through a particularly beautiful hemlock grove. Only a few people live on this road, and one is not particularly friendly (a sign on a tree says "Private Driveway—Keep The Hell Out" with the E shaped like a devil's pitchfork!).

Reach the Delaware at Milford, an attractive little town with a good food store. Then cycle for 10 miles along the river on a one-lane road with a cliff on one side (look for cactus growing on the cliff) and an old railroad track on the other. This is flat, pretty riding, especially in the fall.

Halfway along your river jaunt is Riegelsville. Cross a suspension bridge built by John A. Roebling and Company (the same folks who built the Brooklyn Bridge). This tiny Pennsylvania settlement features stone houses, a connection to the Delaware Canal (which provides about 50 miles of off-road cycling on its towpath, from Yardley to Easton, Pa.), and a few homey restaurants.

Back in New Jersey, continue the river run. In July and August, look for wild raspberries. After crossing Pohatcong Creek, head inland back to Bloomsbury. The route will take you through a long, dark tunnel under a former railroad grade and on a smooth downhill paralleling the Musconetcong River with big views of cornfields and distant hills. Enjoy!

Directions to Starting Point: The route begins at the **eastern end of Main Street in Bloomsbury**. Use Exit 7 of I-78, then go west on Route 173 (right turn). Main Street forks off Route 173 opposite the truck stop (there is a sign for Bloomsbury). Park on the street, near a small park.

Pt.-Pt.	Cume	Turn	Street/Landmark
0.0	0.0	S	**Main St.**, heading into Bloomsbury
0.6	0.6	R	**Church St.** (T)
0.1	0.7	L	Turn at unmarked **Willow Ave.** (first block; store on right corner after turn). Road goes under tall railroad underpass
0.4	1.1		**Pavement ends**
0.2	1.3	R	**Staats Rd.** (T). Road changes name to **Myler Rd.**
2.1	3.4	R	**Sweet Hollow Rd.** (T)
1.4	4.8	S	At stop sign, keeping Little York Tavern on right, onto **Rt. 614 West**
0.3	5.1	BL	**Rt. 631 South**
1.1	6.2	R	**Miller Park Rd.** (dirt road)
1.9	8.1	L	**Javes Rd.** (T). Road changes name to **York St.** as it comes into Milford
1.0	9.1	L	**Mill St.** Turn is just before the T at the busy highway
0.2	9.3	L	**Water St.** (T)
0.1	9.4	R	**Bridge St.** (traffic light; no sign)
0.1	9.5	R	**Church St.** Turn is just past Little Falls Bank. Food store across Bridge St. from turn.
0.1	9.6	R	**Spring Garden St.** Becomes **Rt. 627 North**

Pt.-Pt.	Cume	Turn	Street/Landmark
5.2	14.8	L	**Old River Rd.** Turn is opposite Church Rd. and a church
1.7	16.5	L	**Rt. 627 North** (T). Immediately cross Musconetcong River
0.2	16.7	L	At T, heading toward Riegelsville. Rt. 627 North goes right
0.2	16.9	L	Cross suspension bridge toward Riegelsville, Pa. (*Note:* Walk bikes on walkway; police enforce laws against biking on roadway)
0.2	17.1		**Riegelsville**; two homey restaurants and interesting buildings. Connection to Delaware Canal towpath just before small bridge over canal, on right (steep downhill path, with poison ivy). After visiting, U-turn and return across suspension bridge, walking bikes on walkway
0.3	17.4	L	At T at New Jersey end of bridge, onto **River Rd.** toward Carpentersville
2.7	20.1	R	At T after crossing green bridge over Pohatcong Creek onto unmarked **Creek Rd.** Road going left goes under railroad underpass
1.2	21.3	L	At T to continue on **Creek Rd.** Mountain Rd. goes right
1.2	22.5	L	**Rt. 519** (T; no sign)
0.4	22.9	R	**Rt. 636 East/Municipal Dr.**
1.3	24.2	L	**Rt. 639 East** (T)
2.0	26.2	R	**Rt. 173 East** (T)
0.1	26.3	R	Toward Bloomsbury; cross green bridge over Musconetcong River
0.1	26.4		**Store** on right
0.1	26.5	L	**Main St.** (school on corner; street sign may be turned around)
0.6	27.1		East end of **Main St.** End of route

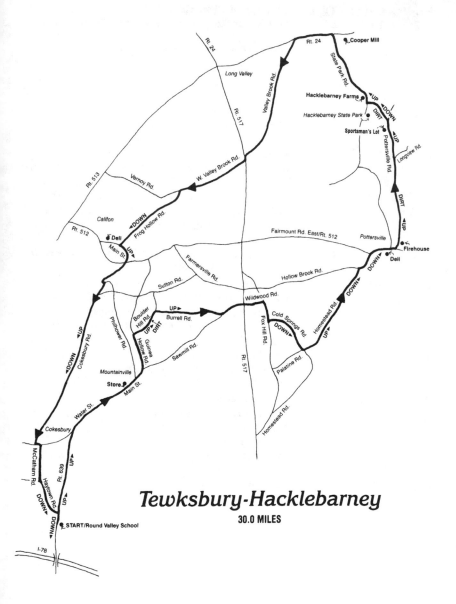

Tewksbury-Hacklebarney

30.0 MILES

Tewksbury-Hacklebarney—30.0 miles

Tewksbury Township is so beautiful that just one route alone won't do it justice. Although this route is hilly, it is one of the most scenic in RIDE GUIDE.

Terrain: Hilly, almost continuously so. Valley Brook Road is gently rolling, but otherwise you're usually going up or down.

Traffic: Incredibly light! Most roads are so narrow that two cars could barely pass each other. But you'll almost never see two cars at the same time, except for one short busy stretch on Route 24.

Road Conditions: Good, for the most part. Boulder Hill Road is hard-packed dirt. The section north from Pottersville to Hacklebarney has quite a bit of dirt or pavement in the process of becoming dirt, some of it rather rough.

Points of Interest: General store in Mountainville; hills and horse farms of Tewksbury; **Hacklebarney State Park**; **cider mill** in Hacklebarney; **Cooper Mill** (interpretive exhibit May-early Oct.; picnic area); pretty back roads scenery.

Thoughts of the roads surrounding Mountainville, Pottersville, and Califon are bound to bring a smile to a cyclist's lips—and a soreness to his or her legs. This tour is one of the hilliest in *RIDE GUIDE*, but also one of the most beautiful. If you've cycled any of the routes in *RIDE GUIDE/North Jersey*, or many of the Hunterdon and Somerset county rides in this book, you should be able to handle Tewksbury's hills. Just don't expect the respite of a merely rolling road until you get to Valley Brook Road.

Leave the Round Valley School and immediately get a taste of things to come with a 1.5-mile climb to Cokesbury. Stop and look over your shoulder at the glorious view of Round Valley Reservoir. This area is explored in the "Round The Valley" route.

From Cokesbury to Mountainville follow the burbling brook on a narrow, tree-shaded road. Mountainville has a country store that makes a nice stopping point.

Follow a different burbling brook out of Mountainville. Climb some hills past some horse farms and a former winery.

Cold Spring Road and Homestead Road heading into Pottersville contain some glorious downhills—enjoy! After Pottersville, the primary direction is up to the Hacklebarney area, and steeply so. When you finally get there (you'll know it by the return of decent pavement), enjoy a cold (or warm) glass of cider in the fall at Hacklebarney Farms.

Ride over to the state park and walk through a pretty gorge on the Black River (no ATBs allowed on the park's trails). You may picnic here, at the cider mill, or at Cooper's Mill, a Morris County park at the northern tip of the route. The mill operates from May to early October; it is fascinating to watch waterpower from the Black River grind flour.

As previously alluded to, enjoy a gently rolling four miles on Valley Brook Road. Frog Hollow is all downhill into Califon, through a beautiful forest and next to a stream. What goes down must ... well, you know the rest. But upon reaching Cokesbury, the major climbs are behind you and it's just about all downhill back to the end point.

Directions to Starting Point: Round Valley School (Clinton Township) is a half mile north of I-78, Exit 20B, on the right.

Pt.-Pt.	Cume	Turn	Street/Landmark
0.0	0.0	R	At end of school driveway, turn right onto **Rt. 639** (no signs). Road becomes **Water St.** in Cokesbury and **Main St.** in Mountainville
3.9	3.9		**Chelsea Kitchen/General Store** on left
0.2	4.1	L	**Guinea Hollow Rd.**
0.5	4.6	R	**Boulder Hill Rd.** (unpaved)
0.6	5.2	R	**Burrell Rd.**
1.2	6.4	L	**Sawmill Rd.** (T)
0.6	7.0	S	Cross Rt. 517 (no signs) at stop sign, onto **Wildwood Rd.**
0.6	7.6	R	**Fox Hill Rd.** (T)
0.1	7.7	L	**Cold Springs Rd.** *CAUTION:* Control your speed on steep, winding downhill
1.3	9.0	L	**Homestead Rd.**
1.4	10.4	R	**Hollow Brook Rd.** (T)
0.2	10.6	R	**Fairmount Rd. East** (T)

Pt.-Pt.	Cume	Turn	Street/Landmark
0.5	11.1		**Deli** on right
0.1	11.2	**L**	Immediately after bridge over Black River onto **unmarked road**. Pass Pottersville Fire Co. on right immediately after turn. **Pavement will end**
2.0	13.2	**BL**	To continue on **Pottersville Rd.** Longview Rd. goes right
0.7	13.9	**BL**	At unmarked fork just past Hacklebarney Sportsman's Lot. Follow signs for Cooper Mill
0.8	14.7	**R**	**State Park Rd.** (T; paved). If you wish to visit **Hacklebarney State Park**, turn **left** here instead and cycle 0.2 miles. Park entrance is on the left. After visiting this park, cycle back to this intersection and continue on the paved road
0.1	14.8		**Hacklebarney Farms** (cider, apples) on left
1.8	16.6	**L**	**Rt. 24** (T). To visit **Cooper Mill County Park**, turn **right** here instead. Mill is on the right in 0.1 miles
0.8	17.4	**L**	**Valley Brook Rd.**
2.1	19.5	**L**	**Rt. 517** (T)
0.1	19.6	**R**	**West Valley Brook Rd.**
2.0	21.6	**L**	**Frog Hollow Rd.**
2.9	24.5	**L**	**Main St.**, Califon. If you need a deli, turn **right** here and go down several blocks. **Rambo's General Store** will be on the right (closed Sunday).
0.3	24.8	**S**	Cross Rt. 512 at stop sign onto **Cokesbury Rd.**
0.4	25.2	**R**	At partially marked fork (after switchback) to continue on **Cokesbury Rd.** Philhower Rd. goes straight
2.2	27.4	**L**	At unmarked T
0.1	27.5	**R**	**McCatharn Rd.**
1.0	28.5	**L**	**Haytown Rd.** (T)
1.1	29.6	**R**	**Rt. 639** (T)
0.4	30.0	**L**	Into **Round Valley School**. End of route

Northern Hunterdon Hillbilly
30.0 MILES

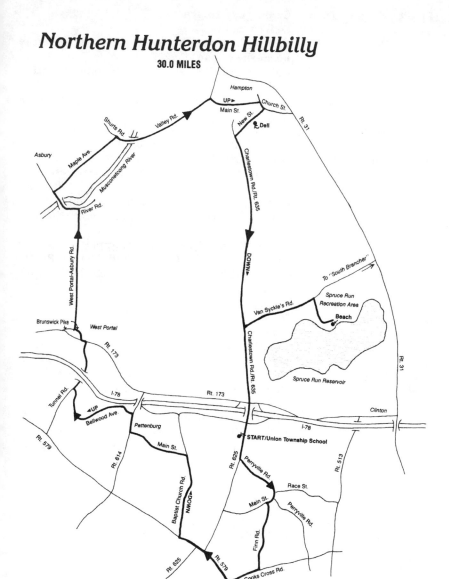

Northern Hunterdon Hillbilly—30.0 miles

If you are one of those cyclists who just loves to climb hills, you'll find good views, quiet back roads, and a reward at the end of this route—a swim in Spruce Run Reservoir.

Terrain: The name says it all. A number of major climbs and descents, otherwise rolling. The sections along the Musconetcong River and Spruce Run Reservoir, however, are flat!

Traffic: Very light. Moderate near Spruce Run.

Road Conditions: Good. No dirt roads.

Points of Interest: Great views, pretty back roads; swimming or relaxing at **Spruce Run Reservoir**.

Bethlehem Township is one of the hilliest communities in this hilly county. This route crosses a few major ridges in order to give you some fine views of surrounding farm country. The ride on West Portal-Asbury Road is particularly noteworthy because it is an exhilarating gradual downhill with a good view of Warren County to the left. Eventually this road leads down to the Musconetcong River, where you'll enjoy several miles of flat cycling through horse country.

The one major town you cycle through is Hampton, which, of course, sits on top of a hill. This is the first deli stop (at a little over 18 miles), so bring enough food and water to last to this point.

After a few more small climbs, descend into the valley containing Spruce Run Reservoir and enjoy a cooling dip. You certainly deserve it!

Note: Ambitious cyclists seeking a longer ride may combine this route with the South Brancher. Exit Spruce Run by going right on Van Syckle's Road (mile 26.6). Pick up the South Brancher cue sheet at mile 24.6. After turning left at Arch Street (mile 27.5), continue straight. Do not turn right at Jerricho Road (mile 27.6). You are now at mile 2.9 of the South Brancher cue sheet. Loop back to Spruce Run via the South Branch of the Raritan River, and then rejoin the Northern Hunterdon Hillbilly cue sheet. This will add 23.7 miles to the distance, for a grand total of 53.7 hilly miles.

Directions to Starting Point: This route begins at the **Union Town-ship School**. Use Exit 12 off I-78. Turn left at the stop sign at the top of the ramp, then left again toward Jutland. Cross the highway and proceed straight about half a mile. The school is on your right.

Pt.-Pt.	Cume	Turn	Street/Landmark
0.0	0.0	R	Exit school onto **Rt. 625**.
0.1	0.1	L	**Perryville Rd.**
0.7	0.8	S	**Main St.** (Perryville Rd. goes left). Before this intersection, beware of railroad crossing on a downhill. Tracks cross road at a sharp angle
0.1	0.9	L	**Finn Rd.**
1.6	2.5	R	**Cooks Cross Rd.** (T)
0.4	2.9	R	**Rt. 579** (T)
1.4	4.3	R	**Baptist Church Rd.** Enjoy superb downhill with great view
1.3	5.6	L	**Main St.**
1.4	7.0	R	**Rt. 614** (T; no sign). Go under one-lane railroad underpass after turn
1.0	8.0	L	**Bellwood Ave.** (toward North Hunterdon Hills VFW). Prepare to climb!
3.2	11.2	R	**Tunnel Rd.** (T; no sign)
1.0	12.2	L	**Rt. 173** (T). *CAUTION*: cars come quickly down the hill from the right, so be careful on this turn
0.0	12.2	BR	Immediate right turn onto **Brunswick Pike** toward Asbury
0.2	12.4	R	Toward Asbury on **West Portal-Asbury Rd.**
2.5	14.9	L	Curve left at the fork by the Musconetcong River. River Rd. goes right. Cross river into Warren County
0.3	15.2	R	**Maple Ave.**
1.3	16.5	R	**Shurts Rd.** (T). Cross river back into Hunterdon County. Road changes name to **Valley Rd.** (no sign)
1.3	17.8	R	**Main St.**, Hampton (T). Prepare to climb
0.7	18.5	R	**Church St.** (T)
0.0	18.5	R	Immediate right onto **New St. (Rt. 635 South)**. **Deli** on left 0.1 mile after turn
0.4	18.9	L	**Charlestown Rd.** (T). Enjoy a downhill as you approach Spruce Run!

Pt.-Pt.	Cume	Turn	Street/Landmark
4.7	23.6	**L**	**Van Syckle's Rd.**
2.0	25.6	**R**	Into **Spruce Run Recreation Area**. Cyclists pay $1 to enter from Memorial Day to Labor Day
0.4	26.0	**R**	Onto **Service Road**, heading toward beach changing rooms
0.1	26.1		Arrive at beach. Enjoy a swim or picnic. Then exit area the same way you came in
0.5	26.6	**L**	At park exit onto **Van Syckle's Rd.** (T)
2.0	28.6	**L**	**Charlestown Rd.** (T)
1.0	29.6	**S**	At stop sign, crossing Rt. 173 and I-78. You are now on **Rt. 625**
0.4	30.0	**R**	Into **Union Township School**. End of route

A pond near the entrance to the Spruce Run Recreation Area. The actual reservoir is a significantly larger body of water.

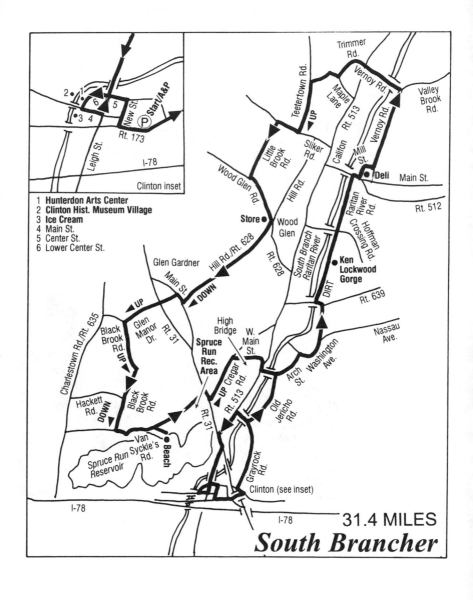

Clinton inset

1 **Hunterdon Arts Center**
2 **Clinton Hist. Museum Village**
3 **Ice Cream**
4 **Main St.**
5 **Center St.**
6 **Lower Center St.**

31.4 MILES
South Brancher

South Brancher—31.4 miles

Members of the Morris Area Freewheelers, a local bike club, were whiz-zing along over the hills and dales of Hunterdon County one fine day. As the club crossed one dale and started climbing another hill, the group passed a quiet road paralleling the South Branch of the Raritan River. It looked a lot flatter than the mountain (Hoffman Crossing Road) the group was about to climb. We said, why aren't we cycling along this lovely river and saving the hills for some other time? So we set out to follow this renowned trout stream for mile after mile. The road we discovered was so beautiful that it renewed our faith in the quality of bicycle touring in New Jersey.

Terrain: Very flat on the northern leg. Some rollers on the way back leaving the river valley. A couple of noticeable leg burners, but nothing a novice can't walk if necessary.

Traffic: Amazingly light—almost non-existent, in fact, except in High Bridge, near Spruce Run Reservoir and two brief runs on Route 31, which has a wide shoulder. (*Note:* New Jersey was "dualizing" Route 31 north of Clinton at presstime. There may be no shoulder during con-struction for 0.7 miles).

Road Conditions: Fair to good. Some patchy pavement. Less than two miles of dirt road through Lockwood Gorge.

Points of Interest: Ken Lockwood Gorge, a breathtakingly beautiful stretch of stream and dirt road; **Califon**, an attractive small riverside town; the classic **country store** in **Wood Glen**; swimming at **Spruce Run Reservoir**; antiquing, gallery hopping, and ice cream eating in **Clinton**.

The South Branch of the Raritan River is a favorite spot for fly-fisher-men. It is not particularly popular for road cyclists because several miles of the streamside road aren't paved. But if you don't mind a little dirt, you can enjoy 11 flat miles along this beautiful river. Bring your camera!

The route starts in Clinton, a pretty town well worth exploring at the end of your ride (the cue sheet lists the specific points of interest at that point). Slip through the outskirts of High Bridge, then immediately join River Road.

In several miles you enter the Ken Lockwood Gorge. This state-owned area is set aside as a fish and wildlife management area. After the first Saturday in April, every bend in the river is occupied by a fisherman in search of the elusive brook trout. Many of them are fly-fishing. If trout enjoy insects, they probably eat very well here because you will notice bugs biting you as you slowly pedal through this dirt road section. It might be a good idea to bring repellant, especially if you plan to linger and take pictures.

Emerging from the gorge, the road becomes paved again and eventually enters Califon. Residents have fought for years to prevent the replacement of the quaint old iron bridge (built in 1887) that serves the town—this keeps traffic volume low and preserves the country atmosphere. A deli is on the corner of Main Street and the river road should you be hungry at this point.

As you reach the northern end of Hunterdon County, the route heads south and west. Because you are no longer in the river valley, expect some of those famous Hunterdon hills. But these are not too bad—only one or two might require walking. The reward, however, is homemade pies and other goodies in the Wood Glen store at the route's halfway point.

A fabulous downhill run takes you to Glen Gardner. The route has been changed since the last edition of this guide to avoid a dangerous unsignaled crossing of Route 31, but the price is a steep climb up from the highway.

The road down to Spruce Run is a true back road, with little development until the southern end. It also has a spectacular downhill, with a view of the reservoir right as it starts getting steep. Control your speed for the stop sign at the bottom of the hill.

A cooling dip at Spruce Run's public beach might feel good now. Or perhaps you might want to watch the sailboarders. End the route in Clinton, where you can enjoy an art center or historic museum on opposite sides of a picturesque mill pond, or perhaps have ice cream at an outdoor riverside cafe.

Directions to Starting Point: The ride starts at the **Clinton A&P**. From I-78 West, use Exit 15. Turn right on Route 173 and proceed 0.7 miles. The A&P will be on your left.

Pt.-Pt.	Cume	Turn	Street/Landmark
0.0	0.0	**L**	Exit A&P onto **Rt. 173 East**
0.4	0.4	**S**	At traffic light, toward Annandale and Washington
0.2	0.6	**L**	At T toward Rt. 31 north
0.1	0.7	**R**	**Grayrock Rd.**
1.4	2.1	**R**	**Old Jerricho Rd.** No street sign! Look for small spring or wellhouse at corner, on property of large old house. If you cross a one-lane bridge, you've gone too far.
0.8	2.9	**R**	**Arch St.** (T)
0.4	3.3	**R**	**Washington Ave.** (T)
0.2	3.5	**L**	Curve left to continue on **Washington Ave.** at firehouse
0.4	3.9	**S**	Nassau Ave. goes right. Road you're on becomes narrow and bumpy and goes uphill. Road becomes **County Rt. 639**
1.0	4.9	**L**	Turn left where main road curves right. Pass a Clinton Twp. parking regulations sign
0.1	5.0	**R**	At unmarked fork. Do not cross one-lane bridge
0.4	5.4		Road becomes **dirt** as it enters **Lockwood Gorge** area
1.8	7.2		**Pavement returns**
0.3	7.5	**S**	Cross Hoffman Crossing Rd. Continue on **Raritan River Rd.**
1.6	9.1	**R**	**Main St.**, Califon
0.0	9.1	**L**	Immediate left onto **Mill St.** Deli (**Rambo's General Store**, closed Sunday) on right after turn
0.2	9.3	**L**	**Vernoy Rd.** (T)
1.7	11.0	**L**	To continue on **Vernoy Rd.** (street sign may be confusing). This is the first left turn after Califon, and it crosses the river immediately
0.5	11.5	**S**	Cross Rt. 513. Road becomes **Trimmer Rd.**
0.7	12.2	**R**	**Maple Lane** (T)
0.4	12.6	**BL**	**Teetertown Rd.** (this will seem like a "straight"). Continue climbing. Brake for stop sign when you start descending
0.6	13.2	**R**	**Sliker Rd.** (T; no sign)
0.5	13.7	**L**	**Little Brook Rd.**
1.3	15.0	**L**	**Wood Glen Rd.** (T; no street sign)
1.0	16.0	**R**	**Hill Rd. (Rt. 628 West). Wood Glen Store** on corner

Pt.-Pt.	Cume	Turn	Street/Landmark
3.2	19.2	**R**	**Main St.**, Glen Gardner (stop sign) (T). *CAUTION*: Control your speed on **Hill Rd.'s** steep descent. Pass through a one-lane railroad underpass and come to the stop sign at the bottom of the hill
0.1	19.3	**L**	Turn onto street with a sign warning of a one-lane bridge (no street sign). Cross old narrow bridge. A playground will be on the left.
0.1	19.4	**S**	Cross Rt. 31 at traffic light. Road becomes **Glen Manor Dr.** Climb a long, steep hill
0.5	19.9	**L**	**Black Brook Rd.** (T) (no signs)
1.1	21.0	**S**	To continue on **Black Brook Rd.** (Hackett Rd. goes right). *CAUTION:* Extremely steep hill begins after you see Spruce Run Reservoir in the distance. Control your speed!
1.5	22.5	**L**	**Van Syckle's Rd.** (T)
1.1	23.6	**R**	Into **Spruce Run Recreation Area.** Cyclists pay $1 to enter from Memorial Day to Labor Day
0.4	24.0	**R**	Onto **Service Road**, heading toward beach changing rooms
0.1	24.1		Arrive at beach. Enjoy a swim or picnic. Then exit area the same way you came in
0.5	24.6	**R**	At park exit onto **Van Syckle's Rd.** (T)
1.5	26.1	**R**	**Rt. 31** (traffic light) (T). Busy road, use shoulder
0.2	26.3	**L**	**Cregar Rd.** Walk your turn across Rt. 31. Climb steeply for a short distance
0.5	26.8	**R**	**West Main St.** (no street sign; turn is immediately before wood-floored bridge with a posted weight limit of 3 tons). Road becomes **Rt. 513 South** in High Bridge
0.7	27.5	**L**	**Arch St.**
0.1	27.6	**R**	**Jerricho Rd.**
0.8	28.4	**R**	**Grayrock Rd.** (no street sign) (T). Cross one-lane bridge
0.3	28.7	**L**	**Rt. 513 South** (T)
0.3	29.0	**L**	**Rt. 31 South** (T). Ride on shoulder
0.7	29.7	**BR**	Toward Clinton. **Spruce Run dam** is on your right
0.8	30.5	**R**	**Lower Center St.** Turn is just after crossing bridge.

Pt.-Pt.	Cume	Turn	Street/Landmark
0.1	30.6	**L**	**Main St. Hunterdon Art Center** is the stone building on the right by the river. You might wish to walk your bike on the sidewalk of the bridge (right turn) to go to **Clinton Historical Museum Village** across the river before returning to Main St. **Clinton Country Store and Eatery** (outdoor riverside ice cream cafe) is on Main Street directly across from this intersection
0.1	30.7	**L**	**Leigh St.** (stop sign)
0.1	30.8	**R**	**Center St.** Pretty houses on this street
0.2	31.0	**R**	**New St.**
0.1	31.1	**L**	**Rt. 173** (T)
0.3	31.4	**L**	Into **A&P parking lot**. End of route

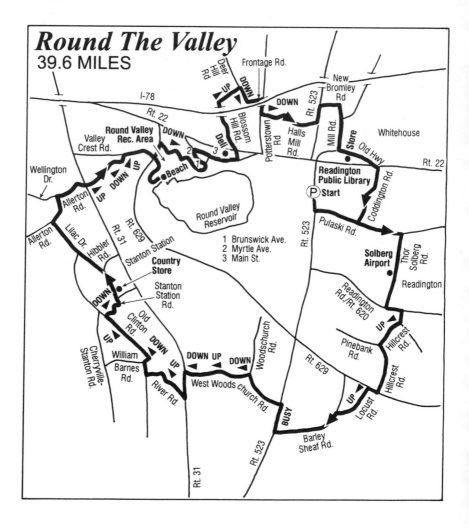

Round The Valley
39.6 MILES

Frontage Rd.

Deer Hill Rd.

UP **DOWN**

New Bromley Rd

I-78

Rt. 22

DOWN

Rt. 523

Blossom Hill Rd.

Round Valley Rec. Area

Valley Crest Rd.

DOWN

Deli

Halls Mill Rd.

Mill Rd.

Store

Whitehouse

Potterstown Rd

Old Hwy

Rt. 22

Wellington Dr.

Beach

UP DOWN UP

Allerton Rd.

Readington Public Library

P **Start**

Coddington Rd.

Round Valley Reservoir

Allerton Rd.

Lilac Dr.

Hibbler Rd.

Rt. 629

Rt. 31

Stanton Station

Rt. 523

Pulaski Rd.

1 Brunswick Ave.
2 Myrtle Ave.
3 Main St.

Solberg Airport

Thor Solberg Rd.

Country Store

Stanton Station Rd.

Readington

DOWN

Old Clinton Rd.

DOWN UP

DOWN UP **DOWN**

Readington Rd./Rt. 620

UP

Cherryville-Stanton Rd.

UP

William Barnes Rd.

River Rd.

West Woods church Rd.

Woodschurch Rd.

Rt. 629

Pinebank Rd.

Hillcrest Rd.

Hillcrest Rd.

BUSY

UP

Locust Rd.

Rt. 523

Rt. 31

Barley Sheaf Rd.

Round The Valley—39.6 miles

Bike clubs (and bike route books) long have made Round Valley Reservoir the centerpiece of cycling routes. This is an old favorite Round Valley route, which, of course, includes a swim at the reservoir's public beach.

Terrain: Gently rolling for the most part, with a few steeper climbs and descents near the South Branch of the Raritan River and again near the reservoir.

Traffic: Light, with a few moderate stretches on numbered highways and by Round Valley Recreation Area. Very heavy during balloon festival.

Road Conditions: Good. Very smoothly paved, for the most part.

Points of Interest: Solberg Airport, site of **annual balloon festival** (third weekend in July); **Stanton Station Country Store** (antiques and country nicknacks); **Round Valley Recreation Area** (swimming); picturesque old highway towns of **Lebanon** and **Whitehouse**.

Magnificent views, woods, and open country are the orders of the day in the area of Round Valley Reservoir. This Hunterdon County water storage lake formerly was a quiet farming valley; creation of the reservoir and the building of I-78 have made the area more residential but it retains its placid beauty.

Cycle east from the Readington Public Library in Whitehouse Station. Pulaski Road is a straight, gently rolling road that connects with Thor Solberg Road. The latter takes you to Solberg Airport, a busy private aviation field and site of an annual balloon festival. The balloons are a beautiful sight at dawn and dusk, when they rise en masse.

Next, ride west toward Stanton through some more pleasant and relatively flat farm country. Approach Stanton Station on a steep downhill road that suddenly crosses an old green iron bridge. The general store next to the railroad sells "country items" and is worth a look.

After crossing Route 31, the route is all uphill, but your reward is a jump in the lake—Round Valley Reservoir, that is. The public beach here is always refreshing, though it tends to be crowded on summer weekends. There is a $1 charge for cyclists to enter during the summer.

After swimming, cycle down a big hill into Lebanon, a quiet, pretty village that was bypassed by Route 22 and I-78. One can easily imagine Pennsylvania-bound Model Ts driving down the main streets of Lebanon or Whitehouse before the highways were built, and the town residents on their porches on summer evenings watching the world go by. The pretty houses in Lebanon and Whitehouse date from the early part of the 20th century (or before) and are in good shape now.

Directions to Starting Point: Readington Public Library is the former Whitehouse Station railroad station. Use Exit 24 off I-78. Head south on Route 523. Proceed 2 miles to Route 22 and turn left. Take an immediate right to continue on Route 523 South. The library is on the right in a half mile, just past the railroad crossing.

Pt.-Pt.	Cume	Turn	Street/Landmark
0.0	0.0	R	**Rt. 523 South**
0.4	0.4	L	**Pulaski Rd.**
3.1	3.5	R	**Thor Solberg Rd.** Look for airport sign
0.9	4.4		**Solberg Airport** on right (site of balloon festival)
0.7	5.1	L	**Readington Rd./Rt. 620** (T; no street sign)
0.3	5.4	R	Onto unmarked road crossing stream (sign for Readington Volunteer Fire Dept.)
0.0	5.4	BR	**Hillcrest Rd.** (fork); toward Readington Volunteer Fire Dept.
0.9	6.3	L	Curve left to continue on **Hillcrest Rd.** (Pinebank Rd. goes right)
1.8	8.1	R	**Rt. 629** (T; no sign)
0.3	8.4	L	**Locust Rd.**
0.8	9.2	S	At stop sign to continue on **Locust Rd.** (no street signs)
0.1	9.3	L	**Barley Sheaf Rd.** (T)
1.4	10.7	R	**Rt. 523** (T; no sign). Busy road: use caution
0.6	11.3	L	**West Woodschurch Rd.**, toward Deer Path Park
0.5	11.8	L	To continue on **West Woodschurch Rd.** Woodschurch Rd. goes straight
1.3	13.1	L	**Rt. 31 South** (T; no sign). *CAUTION:* Intersection at bottom of steep hill. Control your speed! Use shoulder on Rt. 31
0.5	13.6	R	**River Rd.** (first right turn after crossing bridge over South Branch of Raritan River)
0.9	14.5	R	**Old Clinton Rd.** (T)

Pt.-Pt.	Cume	Turn	Street/Landmark
0.3	14.8	R	Curve right to continue on **Old Clinton Rd.** William Barnes Rd. goes left
1.1	15.9	R	**Stanton Station Rd.**
0.6	16.5		Cross green iron bridge
0.1	16.6	L	Onto unmarked **Lilac Dr.** just after crossing railroad. **Stanton Station Country Store** (not a food store) on right after turn
1.0	17.6	L	At stop sign to continue on **Lilac Dr.** Hibbler Rd. goes right
1.6	19.2	R	**Allerton Rd.** (T; no sign)
0.5	19.7	R	To continue on **Allerton Rd.** at T. Wellington Dr. goes left
0.6	20.3	S	Cross Rt. 31 at traffic light
1.3	21.6	R	**Valley Crest Rd.** (T). Look to the left to see a magnificent view before you make the turn!
0.3	21.9	L	**Rt. 629** (T; no signed)
0.1	22.0	R	Into **Round Valley Recreation Area**. Cyclists pay $1 to enter between Memorial Day and Labor Day
0.8	22.8	R	Toward beach
0.2	23.0		Beach (restrooms, changing rooms, refreshments in season). After stopping here, cycle back the way you came in
0.2	23.2	L	At T, toward park exit
0.7	23.9	R	**Rt. 629** (T at park exit; no signs)
0.8	24.7	R	Toward boat launching ramp (road going straight has sign "To Rt. 22")
1.8	26.5	L	**Brunswick Ave.** Turn is shortly after one-lane underpass at bottom of hill leading into Lebanon
0.4	26.9	R	Curve right onto **Myrtle Ave.**
0.1	27.0	R	**Main St.** (T)
0.9	27.9		**Yummy's ice cream/deli** on left in Grist Mill Square
0.2	28.1	L	**Blossom Hill Rd.** No sign! Turn is shortly after passing a two-sided street sign (on left), one side of which says "Main St." and the other side says "Lebanon"
0.1	28.2	S	Cross Rt. 22 at stop sign
1.5	29.7	R	**Deer Hill Rd.** (T)
0.5	30.2	L	Curve left onto unmarked **Frontage Rd.** paralleling I-78

Pt.-Pt.	Cume	Turn	Street/Landmark
0.5	30.7	R	**Potterstown Rd.** (T). Cross over I-78
0.1	30.8	L	**Halls Mill Rd.**
1.9	32.7	L	**Rt. 523 North**
0.4	33.1	R	**New Bromley Rd.**
0.9	34.0	BR	At unmarked fork onto **Mill Rd.**
1.0	35.0	L	**Old Highway** (T). Ride into Whitehouse
0.8	35.8		**Store** on right
0.3	36.1	L	**Rt. 22 East.** Ride on shoulder after carefully crossing both westbound and eastbound lanes of this highway
0.2	36.3	R	**Coddington Rd.**
1.4	37.7	R	**Pulaski Rd.** (T)
1.5	39.2	R	**Rt. 523 North** (T)
0.4	39.6	L	Into **Readington Public Library parking lot**. End of route

Flemington-Raven Rock—39.8 miles

Another section of the Delaware River is explored on this route, which includes the pretty borough of Frenchtown.

Terrain: Gently rolling, with a few longer, steeper hills coming into and out of the Delaware Valley.

Traffic: Light, except moderate to heavy in Flemington.

Road Conditions: Good to excellent, but there are several short sections of dirt road. ATBs may parallel the route on the Delaware & Raritan Canal.

Points of Interest: Green Sergeant's Covered Bridge (only public covered bridge in New Jersey); **Bull's Island** (section of **Delaware & Raritan Canal State Park** with pedestrian bridge to Pennsylvania); **Frenchtown** (riverside cafe, shops); **Flemington** (outlet stores, steam train).

The countryside west of Flemington retains some classic West Jersey rural riding—gently rolling roads, farms, woods, and lots of tranquility.

Start by cycling west and south toward Locktown. Follow the cue sheet closely, as there are few street signs in this part of the route. A pretty white church in Locktown dating to the 1820s marks the end of a long flat stretch of road.

Next, cycle slowly down a dirt road that leads to a pretty view of a stream and waterfall. Follow the stream south (and downhill) to the covered bridge near Sergeantville. According to a plaque by the bridge, the entire span was dismantled in 1961 to make way for a conventional bridge. Public outcry forced the state to rebuild the covered bridge from its original materials.

Head up a hill into Rosemont. It's all downhill from there to Raven Rock on the Delaware, so named for the huge rock cliff perched behind historic houses.

Visit Bull's Island Park. There's a large grassy area good for picnics, and you can walk across the pedestrian bridge to Lumberville, Pa.—a pretty town of old stone buildings and a restored canal lock.

Next, cycle north along the river to Frenchtown. Route 29 has wide shoulders, is smoothly paved, and lightly traveled. Or you can cycle along the parallel Delaware & Raritan Canal (the path is actually on an old railroad line and is smooth as silk, flat, quiet, and bucolic). Look for water cascading over the rocks to your right, especially in the spring.

As you approach Frenchtown, the route takes you onto the D&R Canal then River Road for a close look at the Delaware River. Stop at the Bridge Cafe for a snack and watch the world (and river) go by from their outdoor tables.

Leaving Frenchtown you will climb on Ridge Road, then enjoy flat-to-rolling terrain the rest of the way, with a tremendous 1.2-mile downhill heading into Flemington on Old Croton Road. Flemington features outlet shopping, a famous cut-glass shop and gallery, an old steam passenger train, and beautiful architecture on Main Street, including the 170-year-old courthouse that was the scene of the Lindbergh baby kidnapping trial.

Directions to Starting Point: Robert Hunter School is in Raritan Township just west of Flemington. From the Flemington Circle (junction of Routes 202 and 31), go west on Route 12 toward Frenchtown straight through two more traffic circles. The first left turn past the second circle is Dayton Road. The school is on the right in less than a block.

Pt.-Pt.	Cume	Turn	Street/Landmark
0.0	0.0	**R**	Leaving the parking lot of the Robert Hunter School, turn right onto **Dayton Rd.**
0.1	0.1	**R**	**Rt. 523 South** (stop sign; no street sign)
0.9	1.0	**R**	**Harmony School Rd.**
2.1	3.1	**L**	**Rt. 579** (T; no signs)
0.3	3.4	**R**	**Locktown-Flemington Rd.** (unmarked; turn is first right, in the middle of a curve)
1.2	4.6	**S**	At unmarked intersection just past bridge over stream, to continue on **Locktown-Flemington Rd.**
1.4	6.0	**L**	**Locktown-Sergeantville Rd.** (T; no signs; church on corner)
0.4	6.4	**R**	At unmarked T onto **Pine Hill Rd.**
0.8	7.2	**R**	Onto **Old Mill Rd.** (unmarked). Auto salvage yard on corner. If you miss the turn, road becomes dirt. Old Mill Rd. also **becomes dirt**, so you will lose pavement either way. Use caution going downhill on dirt road

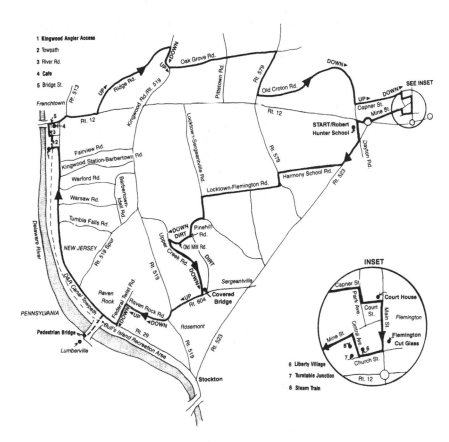

1 Kingwood Angler Access
2 Towpath
3 River Rd.
4 Cafe
5 Bridge St.

Frenchtown

Oak Grove Rd.
Ridge Rd.
Kingwood Rd./Rt. 519
Pittstown Rd.
Rt. 579
Old Croton Rd.
DOWN►
UP►
DOWN►
SEE INSET
Capner St.
Mine St.
UP►
DOWN►
Rt. 12
Rt. 12
START/Robert Hunter School
Dayton Rd.

Rt. 513
Fairview Rd.
Kingwood Station-Barbertown Rd.
Warford Rd.
Barbertown Idell Rd.
Warsaw Rd.
Locktown-Sergeantsville Rd.
Locktown-Flemington Rd.
Harmony School Rd.
Rt. 523
Rt. 579

Delaware River

NEW JERSEY
Tumble Falls Rd.
Rt. 519 Spur
Upper Creek Rd.
Rt. 519
DOWN DIRT
Pinehill Rd.
Old Mill Rd.
DIRT
Sergeantsville
DOWN

PENNSYLVANIA
D&R Canal Towpath
Raven Rock
Federal Twist Rd.
Raven Rock Rd.
UP►
◄DOWN
Covered Bridge
Rt. 604
Rosemont

Pedestrian Bridge
Bull's Island Recreation Area
Rt. 29
UP►
◄DOWN
Rt. 519
Rt. 523
Lumberville

Stockton

INSET
Capner St.
Park Ave.
Court St.
Court House
Main St.
Flemington
Mine St.
Central Ave.
Church St.
8
7
6
Flemington Cut Glass
Rt. 12

6 Liberty Village
7 Turntable Junction
8 Steam Train

Flemington-Raven Rock
39.8 MILES

Pt.-Pt.	Cume	Turn	Street/Landmark
0.4	7.6	**BL**	At unmarked fork after crossing stream
0.2	7.8	**L**	At unmarked T onto the paved **Upper Creek Rd.**
1.8	9.6	**R**	**Rt. 604** (T; no sign). **Green Sergeant's Bridge** (covered bridge) on left at intersection
1.7	11.3	**L**	**Rt. 519 South** (T) in Rosemont
0.2	11.5	**S**	On unmarked **Raven Rock Rd.** toward Raven Rock, where Rt. 519 South goes left. **Cane Farm Furniture** on right at this intersection
1.9	13.4	**L**	**Federal Twist Rd.** (T; no sign)
0.7	14.1	**R**	**Rt. 29 North** (T)
0.5	14.6		**Bull's Island Recreation Area, D&R Canal Park** on left (pedestrian bridge to Lumberville, Pa.). ATB riders can access the canal path northbound at this point
7.9	22.5	**L**	Into **Kingwood Angler Access**
0.1	22.6	**R**	**D&R Canal State Park towpath** (unpaved but smooth)
0.5	23.1	**L**	At first paved road crossing
0.1	23.2	**R**	**River Rd.** (T; no sign; dirt)
0.4	23.6	**R**	**Bridge St.** (no sign, road that comes off bridge from Pennsylvania). **Bridge Cafe** on right after turn
0.1	23.7	**L**	Curve left at corner where sign points right for "To Rt. 29/Lambertville/Trenton"
0.1	23.8	**R**	**Rt. 12 East** (blinker light)
0.3	24.1	**L**	**Ridge Rd.**
3.0	27.1	**R**	**Kingwood Rd./Rt. 519** (T; no sign)
0.9	28.0	**L**	**Oak Grove Rd.**
2.5	30.5	**S**	Cross Pittstown Rd. at stop sign
1.4	31.9	**R**	**Rt. 579** (T; no sign)
1.6	33.5	**L**	**Old Croton Rd.** (street sign is hidden. Turn is by Etzel's Country Restaurant. If you miss the turn, you will hit Rt. 12)
3.4	36.9	**L**	**Capner St.**
1.2	38.1	**R**	**Park Ave.** (stop sign)
0.1	38.2	**L**	**Court St.**
0.1	38.3	**R**	**Main St.** (T)
0.3	38.6	**R**	**Church St.** (traffic light). **Flemington Cut Glass** on left one block before this corner
0.2	38.8	**R**	**Central Ave. Turntable Junction, Liberty Village** and **steam train** at or near this corer
0.1	38.9	**L**	**Mine St.** (T)

Pt.-Pt.	Cume	Turn	Street/Landmark
0.6	39.5	**BR**	At traffic circle onto **Rt. 12 West** toward Frenchtown
0.2	39.7	**L**	**Dayton Rd.**
0.1	39.8	**R**	Into **Robert Hunter School parking lot**. End of route

Delaware & Raritan Canal Lock at Bull's Island

Lighthouse and lighthouse keeper's residence at Sandy Hook

Rides Starting in Middlesex, Monmouth, and Ocean Counties

B
y the sea, by the sea, by the beautiful sea! New Jersey truly has a beautiful Shore. Five of the ten routes in this section head for the ocean from inland points. It is a satisfying feeling to arrive at the Shore on a bicycle, saving the hassles of traffic and parking and feeling healthy. These routes highlight the many back roads to the shore that are free of heavy traffic.

Sandy Hook is approached via the hilly Atlantic Highlands. This ocean playground, served by three *RIDE GUIDE* routes, features clean beaches within sight of New York City, hiking trails through wild holly forests, and the historic buildings of Fort Hancock, a 19th-century munitions testing ground. The Shore towns from Ocean Grove down to Island Beach have unique character, and you'll have plenty of chances to explore them by bike. Inland areas such as Cheesequake Park, Allaire State Park, and the Englishtown flea market are covered here, too.

Manalapan-Millstone is a new *RIDE GUIDE* route that is easy and pleasant. Following flat to gently rolling roads with light to moderate traffic, the cyclist heads west from Monmouth Battlefield toward Roosevelt through truck farms and newer suburbia. The return features roads bordering fields being restored to their 18th-century appearance.

Highland Park-Griggstown is a sensational hybrid ride for those who love peace and quiet amid the hustle and bustle of Central Jersey. Ride 17 miles down the hard-packed dirt of the Delaware & Raritan Canal towpath, enjoying the company of ducks, geese, turtles, and frogs. Enjoy a museum dedicated to the mule tenders who helped run the canal in its heyday, then zip back on the roads in a 13-mile shortcut.

Two rides leave from Allaire State Park, home of Allaire Village, a beautifully restored 19th-century bog iron town complete with steam railroad. **Allaire-Ocean Grove** heads to the pretty Shore towns of Manasquan, Spring Lake, Belmar, and Ocean Grove via quiet, tree-lined roads. The route zigzags inland at the Shore, allowing you to view some of the larger, older shore homes near Spring Lake. Ocean Grove has many interesting gingerbread-type homes, and a two-mile stretch on the return hugs the Shark River.

Cheesequake-Englishtown heads south through relatively flat sections of Middlesex and Monmouth counties, past horse farms and woods, to reach the flea market at Englishtown, an enormous collection of eclectic bargains. Return past lush farm country near Marlboro State Hospital. Cheesequake State Park offers a lake beach and nature trails.

Allaire-Lakewood goes south into Ocean County for a look at Georgian Court College, which is on the grounds of what was once the George Jay Gould estate. The formal gardens are a unique and unexpected treasure. Head back to Allaire via Howell and Freehold township horse country, visiting Turkey Swamp Park.

If you are already at the Shore with your car, try **Island Beach-Point Pleasant.** This route explores the narrow barrier island containing such Shore towns as Seaside Park, Seaside Heights, Mantaloking, and Bay Head. Photographers will want to stop and shoot the many interesting large Shore homes right on the bay or ocean. Lunch is on Manasquan Inlet, with a view of hundreds of boats heading between bay and ocean.

Lincroft-Sandy Hook is the less hilly, shorter approach to Sandy Hook. Ride through the well-to-do communities of Red Bank and Rumson and cross a one-mile bridge over the Navesink River. Enjoy good views of Raritan Bay before crossing over to Sandy Hook.

Monmouth County has large areas of horse farms, and these are the focus of **Freehold-Colts Neck.** Pass by some pretty parks and the photogenic towns of Freehold and Farmingdale on the way back to Monmouth Battlefield, the route's starting point. Enjoy some fresh apple cider in season at a farmstand near the end of the ride.

Sandy Hook Express gets you to the beach in a hurry, following a 9-mile flat paved bike path that starts just off the Garden State Parkway. Hybrid and ATB riders will enjoy the dirt "samplers" from two of Central Jersey's premier mountain biking spots, Huber and Hartshorne Woods. A paved alternate is provided. Enjoy views of river, bay and ocean as you head for the Hook. Return via the "Scenic Route" and Mt. Mitchill overlook.

A challenging, hilly approach to the Shore can be had by cycling **Cheesequake-Sandy Hook.** This challenging 60-miler travels over hilly roads along the Navesink River, then climbs to Twin Lights State Historic Site. Then it's off to "The Hook," the flattest part of the route. Return on beautifully quiet but hilly Kings Highway, through Middletown and suburban Matawan.

Manalapan-Millstone—28.0 miles

*This new route is a good after-work type ride featuring flat to gently roll-
ing type terrain, few turns and moderate traffic.*

Terrain: Flat to rolling.

Traffic: Mostly moderate in this growing area. Somewhat heavier on
Routes 537 and 522.

Road Conditions: Excellent paved roads.

Points of Interest: Small hamlets of **Clarkstown** and **Roosevelt**; scenic area around **Monmouth Battlefield**, including **Owl Haven Nature
Center.**

This is a road rider's delight: A fast route with smooth pavement, few
taxing climbs, few turns, nice truck and horse farms to look at, and
some pretty areas near Monmouth Battlefield.

Burgeoning suburbia is making fast inroads, so there is moderate traffic, especially on Route 537. For the most part, this is still a pleasant
ride. Routes 524 going west and 522 coming back are particularly nice.

The state is attempting to restore the fields along Route 522 to what
they looked like in the late 18th century when the Battle of Monmouth
was fought. For this mile-long stretch you will see nothing but fields
and very old farmhouses. The Owl Haven Nature Center is a pleasant
stop if you wish to bird-watch and hike into these fields, as well as some
woods.

Directions to Starting Point: Monmouth Battlefield State Park is off
Business Route 33, about 2 miles west of Route 9 and 10 miles east of
New Jersey Turnpike Exit 8. Park at any picnic ground. The cue sheet
starts at the first intersection in the park.

Pt.-Pt.	Cume	Turn	Street/Landmark
0.0	0.0		From the first intersection in Monmouth Battlefield State Park, ride down the hill toward the park exit
0.4	0.4	**L**	**Business Rt. 33 East** (T)
0.3	0.7	**R**	**Wemrock Rd.** (traffic light)

Pt.-Pt.	Cume	Turn	Street/Landmark
0.7	1.4	R	**Gully Rd.** (after crossing Rt. 33 freeway)
1.0	2.4	L	**Gravel Hill Rd.** Climb
1.1	3.5	R	**Rt. 537** at stop sign. *CAUTION:* Busy road!
2.2	5.7	S	Cross Rt. 527 at traffic light
0.4	6.1	BR	**Rt. 524/Stage Coach Rd.**
4.7	10.8		Curve right at **Clarksburg General Store** (on right) to continue on **Rt. 524/Stage Coach Rd.**
0.5	11.3	R	**Rt. 571/Rising Sun Tavern Rd.**
2.3	13.6	R	At stop sign to continue on **Rt. 571** in Roosevelt
1.6	15.2	R	At T, where Rt. 571 goes left, onto **County Rt. 1 East**
1.7	16.9	L/R	Turn left where County Rt. 1 goes right and **Prodelin Way** goes left, then make an immediate right onto **Baird Rd.**
1.0	17.9	S	At stop sign, crossing Millstone Rd.
2.3	20.2	S	Cross busy Alt. Rt. 527/Woodville-Smithburg Rd. onto **Lamb Lane**
0.9	21.1	L	At stop sign onto **Woodward Rd.**
0.6	21.7	S	Cross the four lanes of Rt. 33 very carefully at stop sign (you can pause in the median to wait for westbound traffic to clear)
2.1	23.8	S	Cross Rt. 527/Millhurst Rd. at stop sign. You are now on **County Rt. 3**
0.6	24.4		Cross bumpy railroad crossing
0.2	24.6	R	**Rt. 522** (traffic light in Tennent). *CAUTION:* busy
1.1	25.7		**Owl Haven Nature Center** on left (interesting nature trails through fields and woods)
0.5	26.2	R	**Wemrock Rd.** Go under low railroad underpass immediately
1.1	27.3	R	**Business Rt. 33** (traffic light)
0.3	27.6	R	Into **Monmouth Battlefield State Park**
0.4	28.0		First intersection in park. End of route

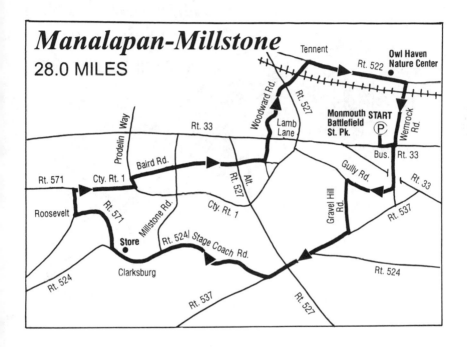

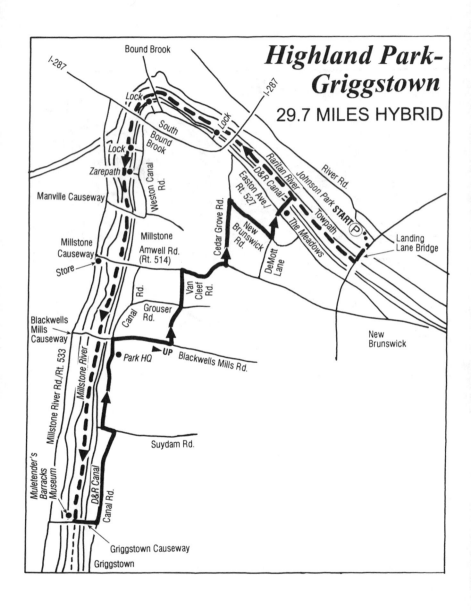

Highland Park-Griggstown

29.7 MILES HYBRID

Bound Brook

I-287

I-287

Lock

South Bound Brook

Lock

Zarepath

Weston Canal Rd.

Manville Causeway

Millstone Causeway

Store

Millstone Amwell Rd. (Rt. 514)

Raritan River

D&R Canal

Easton Ave./ Rt. 527

Johnson Park

River Rd.

START (P)

Towpath

The Meadows

New Brunswick Rd.

DeMott Lane

Landing Lane Bridge

Cedar Grove Rd.

Canal Rd.

Van Cleef Rd.

Grouser Rd.

New Brunswick

Blackwells Mills Causeway

Millstone River

Park HQ

UP Blackwells Mills Rd.

Suydam Rd.

Millstone River Rd./Rt. 533

Muletender's Barracks Museum

D&R Canal

Canal Rd.

Griggstown Causeway

Griggstown

Highland Park-Griggstown—29.7 miles
(Hybrid)

This new route combines road riding with one of the prettiest, flattest ATB trails in the state.

Terrain: Flat as a pancake on the canal towpath. One climb leaving the Millstone Valley.

Traffic: No cars on the path but plenty of cyclists and walkers (watch children) between Blackwells Mills and Griggstown. Moderate traffic on the road return.

Road Conditions: D&R Canal is well maintained, though it can be muddy after rain. Do not go after extensive rain; the path will likely be flooded. Return roads are smooth.

Points of Interest: Mule tenders' museum in Griggstown; views of **canal, Raritan** and **Millstone rivers** on the path. Very energetic cyclists can stop and **rent a canoe** at Griggstown for a paddle on the canal.

The Millstone River Valley is a gloriously quiet strip of Central New Jersey, seeming to be far from the hustle and bustle of the state.

An old relic from the canal era, the Delaware & Raritan Canal is kept free-flowing as a water supply for thirsty residents. The towpath and canal has been a state park since the early 1970s.

This is an ideal ride for a hybrid bike. Although the ATB trail along the canal is linear, this route avoids the out-and-back routine by providing a road return. Because the canal makes a big swing to the north out of the New Brunswick area, following the Raritan River before swinging south alongside the Millstone, the road return is a lot shorter. Cyclists go directly from Griggstown, which is the turn-around point, back to Highland Park, cutting off four miles.

Start by crossing the Raritan River on the once-historic Landing Lane Bridge, which was a narrow, hair-raising 100-year-old crossing for drivers until the state replaced it in the early 1990s. Immediately turn right on the canal towpath, an oasis of tranquility between busy Easton Avenue and the Raritan River.

This section of the canal towpath can be extremely isolated (the next exit is two miles north), so it is suggested that riders go in pairs.

Except for the rough stone spillways, such as the one at the very beginning of the towpath, the D&R Canal towpath is smooth, flat, easy, and fast riding. Some sections have a fair amount of tree roots, others get muddy, but for the most part cyclists make good time.

You will pass several locks along the way which are in excellent shape and very photogenic. Fishermen enjoy trying their luck in the canal near the locks.

The towpath goes under I-287 twice on its upside-down V through central New Jersey. Shortly after the second crossing you ride by Zarephath, a tiny town that consists of a Bible college with one of the most powerful FM radio stations in the state.

After intersecting the Manville Causeway, enjoy one of the nicest canal sections. There are no roads anywhere near, and you will surely see turtles basking on logs in the canal and hear frogs jumping from its banks.

Blackwells Mills is a very attractive crossroads with an old bridge and old canal tenders' home with a lovingly tended garden. Although you may be tired here, hang in for another 3½ miles. Griggstown has a very interesting museum devoted to the long-gone men who built the canal, tended the locks, and ran the barges, first by mule power and then by steam.

Return by quiet roads along the canal, then climb out of the valley and into a rapidly developing section of Franklin Township for the return to Highland Park.

Directions to Starting Point: The ride starts in **Johnson Park** in Highland Park, just outside New Brunswick. Use exit 10 off I-287, marked for River Road/Highland Park. Go south, toward Highland Park (left turn from northbound I-287, right turn from southbound I-287). In about three miles, make a right turn onto Landing Lane and then make another right before the bridge onto the Johnson Park road. Park by the first picnic area, on the left.

If you have an NJ Transit bicycle permit, take the train to New Brunswick. Ride Route 27 North (Albany St.) over the Raritan River, using the sidewalk on the left side of the bridge. Turn left onto the bike path in Johnson Park, and pedal about two miles to the Landing Lane bridge. Turn left, then right onto the towpath (mile 0.2 of the cue sheet).

Pt.-Pt.	Cume	Turn	Street/Landmark
0.0	0.0		Exit parking area and ride dirt paths toward Landing Lane Bridge.
0.1	0.1	R	Cross Landing Lane Bridge on sidewalk
0.1	0.2	R	Right turn after bridge onto **Delaware & Raritan canal towpath.** You are at the very start of the 34-mile main canal towpath section to Trenton. Look for stone mileposts every mile on the right
2.0	2.2		Access to Easton Ave. via footbridge on left.
1.6	3.8		Go under I-287
0.1	3.9		**Five Mile Lock** on left. Road access. Raritan River will not be visible on the right for awhile
1.0	4.9		Path leaves side of canal for short time as you approach South Bound Brook
0.3	5.2		Path returns to side of canal
0.1	5.3		Cross old railroad right of way with rickety bridges going over canal and river. Don't even think about it!
0.2	5.5		Cross busy road which links South Bound Brook and Bound Brook
0.1	5.6		**South Bound Brook Lock** on left. Cross lock gates for port-a-john, road access, post office.
0.8	6.4		Ride under I-287. You are now next to **Millstone River**, one of the few north-flowing rivers in U.S. More tree roots here, and watch for more people using path as well
1.3	7.7		Footbridge over canal to Weston Canal Road on left (no parking available)
0.3	8.0		**Lock** on left (private house behind it). Water filtration station, dam on Millstone River and canoe portage on right
0.6	8.6		Cross road which leads into **Zarephath/Alma T. White Bible College.**
0.6	9.2		Cross Manville Causeway. Nicest section ahead, near no roads, lots of frogs and turtles
2.1	11.3		Cross Millstone Causeway. **Food store** over long bridge to right

Pt.-Pt.	Cume	Turn	Street/Landmark
2.1	13.4		Cross Blackwells Mills Causeway. **State park headquarters**, ranger station and restrooms on Canal Road just south of intersection to left. Very popular towpath section ahead (bikes/hikers/horses)
3.6	17.0	L	Griggstown Causeway. **Mule Tenders' Barracks Museum** on right (open Sat./Sun. 10-4). **Canoe livery** and snacks on the left. After visiting these places, cross the canal. The road return route now begins
0.1	17.1	L	**Canal Rd.**
1.6	18.7	L	To continue on **Canal Rd.** Suydam Rd. goes straight. Water treatment plant on the left
2.0	20.7	R	**Blackwells Mills Rd.** (stop sign). Climb hill
0.7	21.4	L	**Van Cleef Rd.** Toward housing development, but you'll also see a restored windmill that shows this used to be a farm.
0.6	22.0	S	Cross Grouser Rd.
0.9	22.9	R	**Amwell Rd./Rt. 514** (T; no sign. Busy)
0.5	23.4	L	**Cedar Grove Rd.** (traffic light). Bikes often do not trip the traffic light sensor
1.7	25.1	R	**New Brunswick Rd.** (traffic light).
1.3	26.4	L	**DeMott Lane** (traffic lane)
1.0	27.4	S	Cross Easton Ave. at traffic light into small driveway with brown park sign identifying it as "The Meadows")
0.1	27.5	S	Cross bridge over D&R canal
0.0	27.5	R	Onto **D&R Canal towpath**
2.0	29.5	L	At end of path. Cross Landing Lane Bridge on sidewalk
0.1	29.6	L	Onto **path into Johnson Park**
0.1	29.7		Parking lot by picnic area. End of route

Allaire-Ocean Grove—33.3 miles

Many thanks to Ira Wiss for recommending some of the roads used.

Terrain: Flat as a pancake along the shore. A few actual hills to climb inland, but nothing terrifically steep.

Traffic: Surprisingly light inland, considering how close you are to the busy New Jersey Shore. On Ocean Avenue, the main hazard is not traffic but the sheer number of cars backing out of parking spaces. You must be on the alert for this, especially on summer weekends.

Road Conditions: Very smooth. Even the boardwalk in Manasquan is paved! West Hurley Pond Road is somewhat bumpy.

Points of Interest: Beaches from Manasquan to Ocean Grove; **old hotels** and **large homes**, especially in Spring Lake and Avon-by-the-Sea; **Ocean Grove** (gingerbread houses, camp meeting tents, auditorium, ice cream places); **Allaire Airport** (takeoff spot for planes carrying advertising banners for the shore); **Brewer Cemetery** (dating from 1810); **Allaire Village** in **Allaire State Park.**

Ride the best of the Monmouth County Jersey Shore on this route, and enjoy some pleasant, quiet inland areas as well. Be sure to bring sun block, as there is little or no shade on much of this ride.

Start in Allaire State Park. You can spend a good hour or more before or after your ride exploring Allaire Village, a beautifully restored 19th-century bog iron town. Many couples marry in the church here and then ride around the village in a horse-drawn carriage. The hardwood trees in the village make it a photogenic spot in the fall.

Cycle the nine miles to the ocean on quiet, residential roads under large shade trees. The first hint of water comes as you approach Manasquan, where you pass the docks of huge party fishing boats. Cross the tiny drawbridge on Brielle Road, and in a few blocks you'll be hearing the sound of the waves on the Manasquan Boardwalk, which is actually a paved road with houses on one side and the sand on the other. If you wish to start your suntan immediately, ride to the north end and obtain a beach badge (in season). There are restrooms here as well.

The route zigzags inland to view the large homes and hotels of Spring Lake. These are especially striking off-season, looking forlorn and empty and quite cavernous compared to the usual small shore houses. The lake in Spring Lake is pretty and full of swans and ducks, perfect for pictures. You will also ride on Third Avenue, full of chic shops for the shore set.

From Belmar to Ocean Grove make a beeline along the ocean, enjoying the smell of the sea and the sights and sounds of happy people on the beach. You can ride on the boardwalks off-season and early in the morning during the summer. If you are on Ocean Avenue, beware of cars pulling out of diagonal parking spaces. Don't count on them to look for bikes.

In Ocean Grove loop around the auditorium on Pilgrim Parkway and notice the tent houses surrounding it. Ocean Grove was settled as a religious camp-meeting summer community in the 19th century and until recently you could not drive through here on Sunday. Ocean Grove has some interesting stores including Day's, a beautiful garden restaurant and ice cream parlor.

Take a last look at saltwater from pretty Riverside Drive, which goes along the Shark River. Then head inland again. At the top of a hill is Allaire Airport, where you can watch planes taking off trailing the advertising banners you see while at the beach. The scenery as you ride through Allaire State Park is similar to that of the Pine Barrens, with scrub pines and wild blueberries.

Directions to Starting Point: Allaire State Park is on Route 524 in Farmingdale. Use Exit 98 of the Garden State Parkway to I-195 West. Exit 31B off I-195 will take you to Route 524. Make a right at the traffic light, and the park entrance is 1.4 miles on the right. Begin the ride in the parking lot for Allaire Village (a parking fee is charged).

Pt.-Pt.	Cume	Turn	Street/Landmark
0.0	0.0		Exit Allaire Village parking lot
0.3	0.3	R	**Rt. 524 East** (T)
2.2	2.5	S	**Ramshorn Dr.** Rt. 524 curves left
3.3	5.8	L	**Old Bridge Rd.** (stop sign)
0.1	5.9	S	Cross Rt. 70 at traffic light onto **Riverview Dr./ County Rt. 48**
1.7	7.6	R	**Higgins Ave.** (traffic light). **Deli** on left after turn

Allaire-Ocean Grove
33.3 MILES

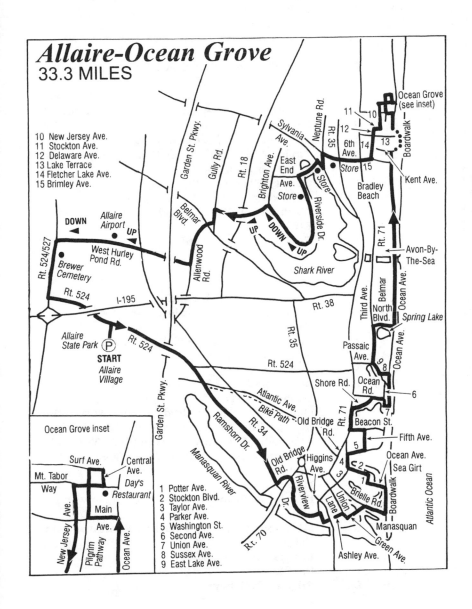

10 New Jersey Ave.
11 Stockton Ave.
12 Delaware Ave.
13 Lake Terrace
14 Fletcher Lake Ave.
15 Brimley Ave.

Garden St. Pkwy.
Gully Rd.
Rt. 18
Brighton Ave.
Sylvania Ave.
Neptune Rd.
Rt. 35

Ocean Grove
(see inset)

11   10
12
6th   14   13
Ave.
Store   15

Boardwalk

Kent Ave.

Bradley
Beach

East
End
Ave.
Store

Store

Riverside Dr.

DOWN   Allaire
Airport   UP

Belmar
Blvd.

UP   DOWN   UP

Rt. 71

Avon-By-
The-Sea

Rt. 524/527

Brewer
Cemetery

West Hurley
Pond Rd.

Allenwood
Rd.

Shark River

Belmar
North
Blvd.   Spring Lake

Third Ave.

Rt. 524   I-195

Rt. 38

Ocean Ave.

Allaire
State Park   Ⓟ   Rt. 524

START
Allaire
Village

Rt. 35

Rt. 524

Passaic
Ave.

9   8

Ocean
Rd.

6

Garden St. Pkwy.

Atlantic Ave.
Bike Path
Rt. 34

Ramshorn Dr.

Manasquan River

Shore Rd.

Old Bridge
Rd.

Rt. 71

Beacon St.

Fifth Ave.

5   Ocean Ave.

Old Bridge
Rd.   Higgins
Ave.

Riverview

4   Sea Girt

2

3   1

Boardwalk

Atlantic Ocean

Ocean Grove inset

Surf Ave.   Central
Ave.
Mt. Tabor   Day's
Way   Restaurant

Main
Ave.

New Jersey Ave.

Pilgrim
Pathway

Ocean Ave.

1 Potter Ave.
2 Stockton Blvd.
3 Taylor Ave.
4 Parker Ave.
5 Washington St.
6 Second Ave.
7 Union Ave.
8 Sussex Ave.
9 East Lake Ave.

Rt. 70

Brielle Rd.

Union
Lane

Manasquan

Green Ave.

Ashley Ave.

7

Pt.-Pt.	Cume	Turn	Street/Landmark
0.1	7.7	L	**Ashley Ave.** toward Manasquan Beach
0.2	7.9	R	**Union Lane** (T)
0.1	8.0	L	**Green Ave.**
0.5	8.5	R	**Brielle Rd.** (T; no street sign). Cross tiny drawbridge
0.6	9.1	L	Onto the paved **Boardwalk** (T; just after crossing First Avenue)
0.4	9.5	L	At end of paved boardwalk, by restrooms and beach-badge sales office, onto **Ocean Ave.**
0.3	9.8	R	**Potter Ave.** (T)
0.1	9.9	L	Curve left onto **Stockton Blvd.**
0.6	10.5	R	**Taylor Ave.** (traffic light). Road changes name to **Parker Ave.**
0.4	10.9	R	**County Rt. 49** (traffic light)
0.0	10.9	BL	At fork after railroad crossing. You are on **Washington St.**, the main street of Sea Girt
0.3	11.2	L	**Fifth Ave.**
0.5	11.7	L	**Beacon St.** (stop sign)
0.3	12.0	R	**Seventh Ave./Rt. 71 North** (traffic light)
0.2	12.2	R	**Shore Rd.**
0.5	12.7	R	**Ocean Rd.** (T)
0.2	12.9	R	Curve right onto **Second Ave.**
0.0	12.9	L	Immediate left onto **Union Ave.**
0.2	13.1	L	**Ocean Ave.** (T)
0.5	13.6	L	**Sussex Ave.**, just past large, domed hotel
0.2	13.8	BR	**East Lake Ave.** (T)
0.3	14.1	R	**Third Ave.**
1.0	15.1	R	**North Blvd.** on north shore of tidal lake
0.7	15.8	L	**Ocean Ave.** (T)
2.9	18.7	R	Opposite Kent Ave. in Bradley Beach, **turn right into parking lot** and then **enter boardwalk** (walk bike if crowded), **turning left. Turn left off boardwalk** to return to **Ocean Ave.** in Ocean Grove
0.3	19.0	L	**Main Ave.**
0.2	19.2	R	**Pilgrim Pathway**, just past Ocean Grove post office
0.1	19.3	R	**Mt. Tabor Way. Day's Garden Restaurant** on right
0.0	19.3	L	**Central Ave.**
0.2	19.5	L	**Surf Ave.**
0.0	19.5	L	**Pilgrim Pathway**

Pt.-Pt.	Cume	Turn	Street/Landmark
0.2	19.7	R	**Mt. Tabor Way**
0.2	19.9	L	**New Jersey Ave.** *CAUTION:* Proceed slowly, as very few intersections have stop signs
0.3	20.2	R	**Stockton Ave.**
0.1	20.3	L	**Delaware Ave.**
0.1	20.4	S	Cross Lake Terrace. Road becomes **Fletcher Lake Ave.**
0.3	20.7	R	**Brimley Ave.** Large church on corner. Road changes name to **Sixth Ave./County Rt. 2** after crossing railroad tracks
0.7	21.4	S	Cross Rt. 35. Store on left
0.4	21.8	L	**Neptune Ave./County Rt. 17**
0.4	22.2	R	**Sylvania Ave.** (stop sign; no street sign). **Store** on left after turn.
0.1	22.3	L	**East End Ave./County Rt. 17** (traffic light)
0.4	22.7	L	**Riverside Dr.** Turn is just past bridge
0.0	22.7	BL	At fork, to continue on **Riverside Dr. Store** (Thomas' Cracker Barrel) on right
2.1	24.8	L	**Brighton Ave.** (T)
0.1	24.9	S	At stop sign, toward **Rt. 18 South.** Climb hill
1.0	25.9	L	**Gully Rd.** (stop sign)
0.2	26.1	R	**Allenwood Rd.**
0.1	26.2	S	At stop sign, crossing Belmar Blvd.
0.9	27.1	R	**West Hurley Pond Rd.** (no sign!)
1.0	28.1	S	Cross Rt. 34 at traffic light
0.6	28.7		**Allaire Airport** on right, at top of hill
2.0	30.7	L	**Rt. 524/547** (T, traffic light)
0.3	31.0		**Brewer Cemetery** (dating from 1810) on left
0.6	31.6	L	**Rt. 524 East** (traffic light)
1.4	33.0	R	**Allaire State Park** main entrance
0.3	33.3		**Allaire Village parking lot.** End of route

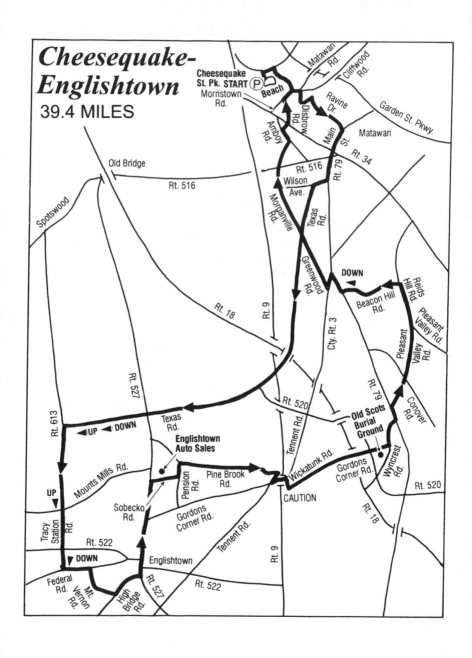

Cheesequake-Englishtown
39.4 MILES

Cheesequake-Englishtown—39.4 miles

Although it may be tough to visit the flea market at Englishtown knowing that you can only buy what you can fit on your bike, it is fun to travel to this well-known attraction by two-wheeled transport, avoiding all the auto congestion.

Terrain: Gently rolling. Flat near Englishtown and on Texas Road near Route 9. A few longer climbs and descents.

Traffic: Moderate overall, but light between the area of Marlboro Psychiatric Hospital and the end of the route. Quite busy near the beginning and end and again near Englishtown.

Road Conditions: Fair to good. Some bumpy pavement conditions near new-home construction.

Points of Interest: Englishtown Auction Sales (the largest flea market you've ever seen, open weekends only); **Old Scots Cemetery**; pretty cycling through Marlboro vegetable farms; **Cheesequake State Park** (swimming, hiking, camping).

Englishtown, New Jersey. The name of this town conjures up many images, depending on who's doing the conjuring. To drag racing fans (and to Baby Boomers who grew up on AM bubblegum radio in New York or Philadelphia in the 1960s or '70s) it's the home of Raceway Park. To bargain fans, including every church group within 150 miles that can charter a bus, it means Englishtown Auction Sales.

For cyclists, the area around Englishtown means flat roads, sandy soil, horse farms, and woods. It also means traffic on the weekend as flea market and drag racing aficionados head to their meccas. You won't pass Raceway Park on this route, but you will visit Englishtown Auction Sales, and you may find yourself becoming a bargain fan. Knowing that you must fit your purchases on your bike will prevent overspending, however!

This area has experienced heavy suburban growth in the decade since *RIDE GUIDE/Central Jersey* first was published. Expect traffic and less woods than before. But there are still some pleasant roads along the way.

The starting point has been relocated into Cheesequake State Park to avoid the hassles of police ticketing cyclists who park at the commuter lot right off the Garden State Parkway.

Start by cycling out of the Cheesequake area through the pleasant town of Matawan. Then head southwest on Texas Road, a nine-mile straight path through rolling hills and woods and housing developments. The first stretch includes no less than four auto junkyards (and their accompanying dogs), but it really is rather scenic in an interesting way.

Route 613 offers a climb. For energy, look for wild grapes growing by the side of the road—ripe for the picking in September.

Approach Englishtown via Mt. Vernon Road, which passes a large, beautifully manicured horse farm. Be careful navigating around stopped traffic in downtown Englishtown. You will be traveling faster than cars on busy flea market mornings.

Englishtown Auction Sales is a half mile long by several hundred yards wide, and you could spend a whole day browsing the booths and eating the food. No matter how long you plan to stay, be sure you bring a very sturdy lock and secure your bike to a good post, tree, or fence. Otherwise someone might be offering your trusty steed for sale before you know it!

The next six miles from Englishtown to Marlboro pass through developing or developed residential areas. When you get to the Old Scots Burial Ground, the roads quiet down and the scenery become more rural. This graveyard dates from 1727 and is the burying place of Rev. John Boyd, the first minister ordained by the first Presbytery of America.

Explore Cheesequake State Park at the end of your ride. Besides having a nice bathing beach on a lake, this park has interesting hiking and nature trails, and an ATB trail. The area borders southern and northern New Jersey ecosystems, with plant life common to both areas.

Directions to Starting Point: Cheesequake State Park is located off of Garden State Parkway Exit 120. Turn right at the top of the ramp. Make a right turn at the first traffic light onto Cliffwood Road, then turn right at the next traffic light onto Gordon Road. Follow the signs to the park entrance, then follow the signs to the lake beach parking area.

Pt.-Pt.	Cume	Turn	Street/Landmark
0.0	0.0		Exit lake parking area the way you drove in
0.2	0.2	R	Toward park exit
0.1	0.3	R	Toward park exit
0.2	0.5	R	Toward park exit, and out of park
1.1	1.6	L	At traffic light onto **Matawan Rd.**
0.3	1.9	R	**Ravine Dr.** (stop sign)
1.4	3.3	R	**Main St.** (T)
0.5	3.8	S	Cross Rt. 34 at traffic light
0.3	4.1	S	Cross Rt. 516 at traffic light. You are now on **Rt. 79 South**
0.4	4.5	R	**Wilson Ave.**
0.1	4.6	BL	At first fork, onto unmarked **Texas Rd.** (sign in center of fork for "Basilian Fathers of Mariapoch")
4.3	8.9	S	Cross Rt. 9 at traffic light. *CAUTION:* Next 2.8 miles are busy on weekends. Road is very narrow, with no shoulders and guardrail immediately next to pavement
2.8	11.7	S	Cross Rt. 527 at traffic light
1.8	13.5	L	**Rt. 613 South** (T)
3.7	17.2	S	Cross Rt. 522 at stop sign onto **Tracy Station Rd.**
0.3	17.5	L	**Federal Rd.** (T)
0.7	18.2	R	**Mt. Vernon Rd.** Turn is easy to miss. If you pass the English-Tudor style townhouses (on left), you've gone too far
0.7	18.9	L	**High Bridge Rd.** (T)
0.6	19.5	BL	**South Main St.** (T). Heavy traffic on flea market mornings
0.6	20.1	L	Curve left to continue north on **Rt. 527**
0.8	20.9	R	**Sobecko Rd. Englishtown Auction Sales** on left for entire length of this road
0.5	21.4	L	**Pension Rd.** (T)
0.3	21.7	R	**Pine Brook Rd.**
1.3	23.0	S	Cross Pease Rd. at stop sign
1.2	24.2	R	**Rt. 9 South** (T)
0.1	24.3	R	Ramp for **Gordons Corner Rd.**
0.1	24.4	L	At T, following signs for Rt. 9 North/The Amboys, crossing over Rt. 9. *CAUTION:* This is a very busy intersection, with cars coming at you from many directions

Pt.-Pt.	Cume	Turn	Street/Landmark
0.1	24.5	**BR**	At fork after crossing highway
0.0	24.5	**L**	Immediate left after fork onto **Wickatunk Rd.** Road changes name eventually to **Gordons Corner Rd.**
2.3	26.8	**S**	Cross Rt. 520 at stop sign
0.6	27.4		**Old Scots Burial Ground** on right
0.1	27.5	**L**	**Wyncrest Rd.** (T)
0.6	28.1	**L**	**Rt. 79** (T; traffic light)
0.1	28.2	**R**	**Pleasant Valley Rd.**
1.0	29.2	**S**	Cross Conover Rd. at stop sign
1.3	30.5	**L**	**Reids Hill Rd.** Pleasant Valley Rd. goes right
0.6	31.1	**L**	**Beacon Hill Rd.**
1.8	32.9	**R**	**Rt. 79 North** (T)
0.6	33.5	**L**	**County Rt. 3** (traffic light) toward Tennent and Millhurst
0.2	33.7	**R**	**Greenwood Rd.**
0.6	34.3	**S**	Cross Texas Rd. at stop sign. Road will change name to **Morganville Rd.**
1.6	35.9	**S**	Cross Matawan/Old Bridge Rd. (Rt. 516) at traffic light
0.3	36.2	**L**	At unmarked T
0.6	36.8	**R**	**Disbrow Rd.**
0.3	37.1	**S**	Cross Rt. 34 at traffic light
0.4	37.5	**R**	At unmarked T
0.3	37.8	**S**	Toward Cheesequake Park. Do not turn toward Garden State Pkwy.
0.5	38.3	**BR**	At entrance to apartments, to continue toward park
0.6	38.9	**L**	At T past park gate toward Hook's Lake
0.2	39.1	**L**	Toward Lake/Picnic Area
0.1	39.2	**L**	Toward Lake
0.2	39.4		**Lake** (swimming area; picnic grove). End of route

Allaire-Lakewood—40.3 miles

Cycle south from Allaire State Park into Ocean County, then return to Monmouth County to enjoy the horse country near Turkey Swamp Park.

Terrain: Flat to gently rolling. Just enough challenge to keep your shift lever fingers from falling asleep.

Traffic: Light to moderate. Heavier near Lakewood.

Road Conditions: Good. One stretch of dirt road heading into Turkey Swamp Park.

Points of Interest: Georgian Court College (former estate of George Jay Gould; huge formal gardens, marble sculptures and large mansions); **Turkey Swamp Park** (lake for picnics and boating); **Allaire State Park** (**Allaire Village** historic restoration and steam railroad, off-road cycling). For off-road cyclists, the entrance to a 5-mile trail loop around Manasquan Reservoir is near this route as well.

Lakewood was a popular resort area in the late 19th and early 20th centuries. George Jay Gould, son of railroad magnate Jay Gould, built an enormous estate here starting in 1896. The estate was modeled after an English manor in the Georgian period. In 1924 the Sisters of Mercy of New Jersey bought the estate and founded Georgian Court College. Because of its unusual history, the college has exceptionally beautiful grounds and is the centerpiece of this ride.

Start by pedaling south out of Allaire State Park. On Hospital Road, you will pass the parking lot which is the starting point for miles of off-road riding—if you don't mind sandy trails.

The roads roll as you pass through several river valleys. The terrain then flattens out and the scenery appears similar to areas of the Pine Barrens, all sandy soil and short, thin trees.

Enter Lakewood on Seventh Street and pedal down Clifton Avenue for refreshments and a look at the "historic downtown" of this former resort community. Then head west alongside Lakewood's lake, called Carasaljo after George Jay Gould's daughters.

Turn right at Lakewood Avenue to visit Georgian Court College. You might wish to stop at Kingscote, the Administration Building (corner of Lakewood and Seventh Street), to get information on the campus. Be sure to look for the amazing Apollo Fountain in the center of the formal gardens. Don't get lost in the formal garden's boxwood maze (the first garden you see as you enter through the gates opposite the Administration Building).

Back on the bike, continue along Lake Carasaljo, then head north back into Monmouth County. Howell and Freehold townships are known for their horse farms. Traffic is usually light along these beautiful roads, so relax and enjoy. Turkey Swamp Park, run by Monmouth County, has a pretty lake with loud ducks and geese. Boat rentals and picnic tables are available.

Upon return to Allaire State Park, be sure to visit Allaire Village, the beautifully restored 19th-century bog iron town. Ride the steam train whose loud whistle is audible throughout the park, and visit the blacksmith shop and old carriage house.

Directions to Starting Point: Allaire State Park is on Route 524 in Farmingdale. Use Exit 98 of the Garden State Parkway to I-195 West. Exit 31B off I-195 will take you to Route 524. Make a right at the traffic light, and the park entrance is 1.4 miles on the right. Begin the ride in the parking lot for Allaire Village. There is a parking fee.

Pt.-Pt.	Cume	Turn	Street/Landmark
0.0	0.0		Exit the parking lot of Allaire Village
0.3	0.3	R	**Rt. 524 East** (T)
1.4	1.7	R	**Hospital Rd.**
1.1	2.8		Entrance to multi-use (off-road cycling) trails at parking lot on the right
0.6	3.4	S	Cross Rt. 21/Squankum Rd. onto **Easy St.** (stop sign)
0.2	3.6	S	Cross Rt. 549 (stop sign)
0.2	3.8	L	**Newton's Corner Rd.** (stop sign)
0.8	4.6	S	Cross Lakewood-Allenwood Rd. (stop sign)
0.4	5.0	R	**Ramtown-Greenville Rd.** Becomes **Ridge Ave.** near the next direction
2.3	7.3	S	Cross Rt. 526 at traffic light. Road becomes **Seventh St.** as you enter Lakewood

40.3 MILES
Allaire-Lakewood

Pt.-Pt.	Cume	Turn	Street/Landmark
2.4	9.7	L	**Clifton Ave.** Restaurants and food stores are located in downtown **Lakewood**, which you will pass through shortly
0.3	10.0	R	**Second St.** (second light)
0.1	10.1	S	Cross Rt. 9 at traffic light
0.2	10.3	R	**Lake Rd.** (T)
0.3	10.6		Turn **right** at Lakewood Ave. to visit **Georgian Court College** (Administration Building on right in two blocks; campus entrance on left). Then cycle back to **Lake Road** and turn **right**
0.5	11.1	L	At fork at end of grounds of Georgian Court College to continue on **North Lake Dr.** (no sign)
1.0	12.1	R	**Hope Chapel Rd.** (T; street sign here identifies street as Hope Rd.)
0.6	12.7	R	**West County Line Rd./Rt. 526** (traffic light). *CAUTION:* Busy road
0.2	12.9	L	**Kent Rd.** (toward Freehold)
1.5	14.4	R	**Lanes Mill Rd.**
0.3	14.7	S	Cross Rt. 9 at traffic light
0.7	15.4	L	**Maxim-Southard Rd.** (stop sign)
1.8	17.2	L	**Oak Glen Rd.**
1.2	18.4		Cross over I-195. If you wish to ride the multi-use trail around **Manasquan Reservoir**, turn **left** shortly after crossing I-195 onto **Windeler Road**. The parking lot by the trail entrance will be on the right in 0.5 mile
0.8	19.2	L	**Manassa Rd./County Rt. 21**
0.9	20.1	L	**Peskin Rd.** (T)
0.3	20.4	L	At fork to continue on **Peskin Rd.** Casino Rd. goes right
1.2	21.6	S	Cross Georgia Tavern Rd. at stop sign. Road becomes **Lemon Rd.**
0.4	22.0	L	**West Farm Rd.** (stop sign)
1.5	23.5	S	Cross Rt. 9 at traffic light. **Deli** on right at corner
2.3	25.8	S	Cross Jackson Mill Rd./County Rt. 23 at stop sign. You are now on **Georgia Rd./County Rt. 53**
1.0	26.8	L	Into **Turkey Swamp Park** (dirt road)
0.4	27.2	L	Toward office. Picnic area by lake. Then U-turn and return the way you came into the park

Pt.-Pt.	Cume	Turn	Street/Landmark
0.3	27.5	L	At park exit onto paved, unmarked **Georgia Rd.**
0.9	28.4	R	**Stone Hill Rd.**
0.9	29.3	S	Cross Jackson Mill Rd. Road changes name to **Bergerville Rd.**
1.4	30.7	S	Cross Rt. 9 at light. Road becomes **Casino Dr.**
3.2	33.9	L	**West Farm Rd.** (stop sign)
0.8	34.7	R	**Squankum-Yellowbrook Rd./Rt. 524A** (stop sign)
4.0	38.7	S	**Rt. 524 East** (traffic light)
1.3	40.0	R	Into **Allaire State Park** main entrance
0.3	40.3		**Allaire Village parking lot.** End of route

Island Beach-Point Pleasant

41.4 MILES

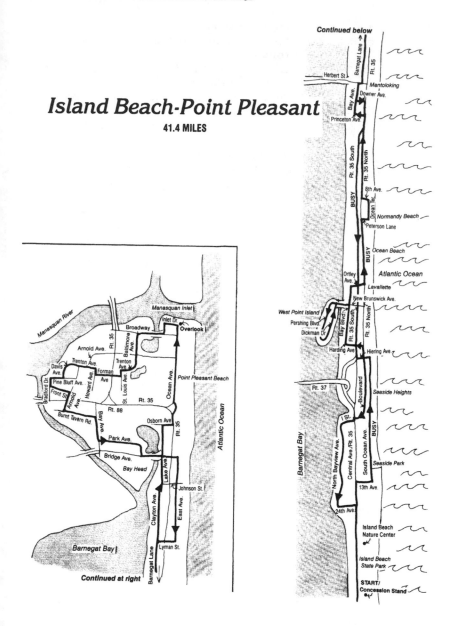

Island Beach-Point Pleasant—41.4 miles

This route is the perfect spin to warm you up for hours of volleyball, surf and sand!

Terrain: Sea level all the way. The only reason you may need your gears is because of the wind (which can blow hard near the ocean, often in your face).

Traffic: In summer season, traffic can be quite heavy, especially on Route 35. Quiet on side roads before Memorial Day and after Labor Day.

Road Conditions: Mostly smooth, with occasional sandy spots after wind-storms. No unpaved sections, except an optional boardwalk (bumpy wood).

Points of Interest: Island Beach State Park (beach, nature preserve); New Jersey Shore amusements in **Seaside Heights**; good boat viewing at **Manasquan Inlet** in Point Pleasant.

Seaside Heights is the town that comes to mind when many people hear the words "Jersey Shore." The crowds of teeny-boppers, games of chance, boardwalk amusements, huge waterslides, and miniature golf courses—they're all there in this oceanfront resort town that is one part of this route.

Start by cycling out of Island Beach State Park, which has no board-walk, but a great clean beach and miles of sand dunes that look the same way they did when the Indians annually came here to gather shellfish.

On the way out, stop at the Island Beach Nature Center, a very interest-ing little nature museum with an interpretive walk through the sand dunes. Signs point out cacti, beach plums and other plants that grow at the shore as you stroll a narrow boardwalk that seems very far from civilization.

Next, head north toward Point Pleasant through shore towns both busy and quiet, large and small, catering to the wealthy or to the middle class. The route takes you along the boardwalk through Seaside Park, then by the boardwalk amusements in Seaside Heights. Try to keep your eyes on the road when you pass the enormous waterslide, big as a five-story building, in Seaside Heights.

Ride along Barnegat Bay in Lavallette, and tour West Point Island, a residential enclave of bayside houses with unusual roofs and shapes.

The barrier island is so narrow through Ocean Beach, Chadwick, and Normandy Beach, there are few parallel roads and you will be forced to ride on Route 35 most of the way. There is a shoulder, but be careful and watch for cars entering from side streets.

Mantaloking and Bay Head offer some quiet parallel roads with great views of the bay. The final northbound segment is in Point Pleasant. Buy lunch at one of the many eateries along Ocean Avenue, and enjoy a break at Manasquan Inlet, where you can watch hundreds of boats cruising between bay and ocean.

Leaving Point Pleasant, ride by the colorful commercial and party fishing boat fleet that calls this borough home port. More bayside back roads bring you to downtown Bay Head, which has several interesting antique and nicknack stores. Look for the miniature lighthouse in the park in Bay Head.

Then it's back to Island Beach via the same towns you passed through on the way up. If you are riding in summer, the prevailing wind is often from the south and you will find great challenge in the return trip. 'Nuff said—if you're riding with a companion, stay close behind his or her wheel for the easiest ride, but out of courtesy take the front once in a while!

If you have energy upon returning to Island Beach, cycle an additional four miles south through the park to explore a bird blind that looks out onto Barnegat Bay (a short hike from the road is required).

Directions to Starting Point: Island Beach State Park is three miles south of Seaside Heights, which, in turn, is seven miles east of Toms River. Take Exit 82 off the Garden State Parkway and follow Route 37 East. In seven miles, after crossing the bridge over the bay, bear right toward Island Beach. The entrance to the park is in three miles. The ride starts at the first concession stand/beach, which is a left turn 3.5 miles past the entrance toll booth. Note that if you wish to drive to the park, plan to arrive by 10 a.m. on busy summer weekends. The gates are closed (to cars) when the park fills up.

Pt.-Pt.	Cume	Turn	Street/Landmark
0.0	0.0	**R**	Exit the parking lot from the first concession stand and turn right toward the park exit
2.3	2.3		**Island Beach Nature Center** on right; boardwalk through dunes, museum
1.1	3.4	**S**	Exit park onto **Rt. 35**
0.7	4.1	**R**	**13th Ave.** (first right turn after entering Seaside Park)
0.2	4.3	**L**	**South Ocean Ave.** (T). Or ride on the boardwalk (closed to bikes after early morning hours in the summer). Road and boardwalk continues into Seaside Heights. Watch for cars pulling out of parking places in Seaside Heights
2.5	6.8	**L**	Curve left onto **Hiering Ave.**
0.1	6.9	**R**	At first stop sign onto **Boulevard**
0.1	7.0	**S**	Merge onto **Rt. 35.** Busy road—use shoulder
0.1	7.1	**L**	**Harding Ave.** Turn is in several blocks
0.1	7.2	**S**	Use caution crossing Rt. 35 southbound at stop sign
0.3	7.5	**R**	**Bay Blvd.**
1.2	8.7	**L**	**New Brunswick Ave.**, toward West Point Island
0.1	8.8	**R**	At fork as you enter island. You will be on **Pershing Blvd.**
0.9	9.7	**L**	At unmarked T onto **Dickman Dr.**
0.7	10.4	**R**	Curve right over bridge onto **New Brunswick Ave.** (unmarked), leaving West Point Island
0.1	10.5	**L**	**Bay Blvd.** (stop sign)
0.8	11.3	**R**	**Ortley Ave.** (toward Mantaloking and Point Pleasant)
0.1	11.4	**L**	**Rt. 35 North** (second intersection). *CAUTION:* Busy road. Watch for traffic entering from side roads!
1.5	12.9	**R**	**Peterson Lane** (first street upon entering Normandy Beach)
0.1	13.0	**L**	**Ocean Terrace** (T)
0.4	13.4	**L**	Curve left onto **8th Ave.**
0.1	13.5	**R**	**Rt. 35 North** (T)
1.2	14.7	**L**	**Princeton Ave.** (turn is shortly after both directions of Rt. 35 merge together on one road)
0.1	14.8	**R**	Curve right onto **Bay Ave.**
0.3	15.1	**R**	**Herbert St.** (T; no signs)

Pt.-Pt.	Cume	Turn	Street/Landmark
0.1	15.2	L	Immediate left onto **Barnegat Lane**. Road changes name to **Clayton Ave.**
1.6	16.8	R	Curve right onto **Johnson St.**
0.1	16.9	L	**Lake Ave.**
0.9	17.8	R	**Osborn Ave.** (T)
0.1	17.9	L	**Main Ave./Rt. 35** (stop sign)
0.0	17.9	BR	Bear right immediately where the sign says "U-Turn"
0.2	18.1	R	At stop sign onto **Ocean Ave.** toward Point Pleasant. Food available at delis and restaurants along the way
1.7	19.8	L	Curve left onto **Inlet Dr.** View of **Manasquan Inlet** at this corner (good outdoor lunch spot; public restrooms available)
0.3	20.1	R	**Broadway** (T)
0.4	20.5	L	**Baltimore Ave.** (traffic light). Becomes **Trenton Ave.**
0.9	21.4	L	**St. Louis Ave.**
0.1	21.5	R	**Forman Ave.** (first stop sign)
0.5	22.0	R	**Howard Ave.** (T)
0.1	22.1	L	**Trenton Ave.** (T)
0.2	22.3	S	Trenton Ave. merges with Arnold Ave. Continue straight on **Trenton Ave**. when Arnold Ave. goes left
0.2	22.5	L	Curve left onto **Davis Ave.**
0.1	22.6	R	**Pine Bluff Ave.** (T)
0.2	22.8	L	**Bradford Dr.** (T)
0.1	22.9	L	**Front St.**
0.2	23.1	R	**Arnold Ave.** (T)
0.1	23.2	S	Cross Rt. 88 at traffic light
0.2	23.4	L	**Burnt Tavern Rd.** (T)
0.6	24.0	R	**Bay Ave.** (T)
0.3	24.3	L	**Park Ave.** (turn is the street before the traffic light)
0.5	24.8	L	**Bridge Ave.** (stop sign). This takes you through downtown Bay Head (interesting shops)
0.2	25.0	R	**East Ave.** (stop sign; street past Rt. 35)
1.4	26.4	R	Curve right onto **Lyman St.**
0.1	26.5	L	**Barnegat Lane** (second stop sign)
0.8	27.3	R	At T onto unmarked **Herbert St.**
0.0	27.3	L	Immediate left onto unmarked **Bay Ave.** (do not cross bridge)

PtPt.	Cume	Turn	Street/Landmark
0.2	27.5	**L**	**Downer Ave.** (road ahead becomes one-way the wrong way)
0.1	27.6	**R**	**Rt. 35.** *CAUTION:* Long stretch of busy road
6.3	33.9	**BL**	On **Central Ave.** toward Seaside Heights where Rt. 35 and "To Rt. 37" go right
0.1	34.0	**L**	**Hiering Ave.** (first turn past traffic light)
0.1	34.1	**R**	**Boulevard** (stop sign)
1.4	35.5	**L**	**Rt. 35**
0.1	35.6	**R**	**I St.**
0.1	35.7	**L**	Curve left onto **North Bayview Ave.**
1.8	37.5	**L**	Curve left onto **24th Ave.**
0.3	37.8	**R**	**Central Ave.** (stop sign)
0.1	37.9	**S**	Enter **Island Beach State Park** (bikes are free and can enter even when gates are closed to cars)
3.5	41.4	**L**	First concession stand. End of route

Lincroft-Sandy Hook

43.0 MILES

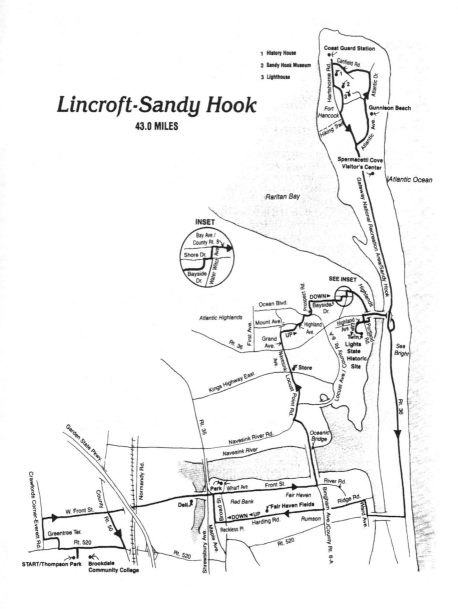

Lincroft-Sandy Hook—43.0 miles

For cyclists who wish to visit Sandy Hook but don't want to ride sixty somewhat hilly miles or deal with dirt, we present this relaxing tour to the beach. This route also explores historic Fort Hancock at the northern tip of Sandy Hook.

Terrain: Rolling overall. Quite hilly in Atlantic Highlands and flat on Sandy Hook.

Traffic: Moderate, somewhat busier in Red Bank. Route 36 in Sea Bright is quite busy in summer.

Road Conditions: Generally good. No dirt.

Points of Interest: Pretty views of the **Navesink River** as you head through the pleasant shore communities of Red Bank and Fair Haven; **antique stores** in Red Bank; **Twin Lights State Historic Site**; Sandy Hook (**Gateway National Recreation Area**) including **Spermacetti Cove Visitor's Center**, **Gunnison Beach** and **Fort Hancock Historic Area**; **Fair Haven Fields** (nature trails); **Brookdale Community College** (several annual festivals); **Thompson Park** (rose garden, mountain biking trails).

The peninsula of Jersey Shore land between the Navesink and Shrewsbury Rivers contains the pretty and rather well-to-do towns of Red Bank, Fair Haven, and Rumson. Straight, gently rolling roads with wide shoulders and lots of shade trees will be your bike avenues to and from the ocean playground of Sandy Hook.

Start at Thompson Park, a Monmouth County facility known by many wedding photographers for its rose garden. Soon you will see pleasure boats tied to the piers lining the headwaters of the Navesink River, which is not really a river but rather a salt-water inlet of the ocean.

Red Bank has some interesting antique stores and a nice park overlooking the river, site of an occasional food festival or concert. After riding east through Fair Haven, turn north and cross the river on the mile-long Oceanic Bridge. Next, head to the Highlands, a hilly part of the Jersey Shore that will test your legs and your lowest gears.

The ride along Bayside Drive, under Ocean Boulevard and closer down to Raritan Bay, is interesting and unique. Modern homes are set back in the hills under the trees, and in between cyclists can catch breathtaking views of the bay, Sandy Hook, the Verrazano-Narrows Bridge, and the New York skyline on a clear day.

Back to more familiar-looking flat Jersey Shore scenery, pedal along an endless chain of seafood eateries and charter fishing boat berths enroute to Twin Lights. The climb to the lighthouse is worth it—the state historic site has an interesting lifesaving museum, a barn housing the original lighthouse lens, and a grassy knoll with a great view of the whole northern Shore area.

After visiting Twin Lights, head out the sandy peninsula known as Sandy Hook. Gunnison Beach is the most familiar swimming area for cyclists because there are trees to lock your bikes very close to the beach, and no big parking lots. If you like to sunbathe *sans* clothing, turn right and walk just a few feet past the sign warning of the start of the nude beach. This is one of the few nude beaches on federal land and one of the biggest and most popular such places on the East Coast.

Circle around the remains of Fort Hancock, an important 19th-century army post and ammunition proving ground. Some stops you might wish to make include History House (an 1890s lieutenant's residence), Sandy Hook Museum, and Spermacetti Cove Visitor's Center, which has interesting exhibits on barrier island flora and fauna. The first two attractions are open weekends only, 1 p.m. to 5 p.m. The Visitor's Center is generally open 10 a.m. to 5 p.m., and occasionally offers tours of the holly forest on the bay side of Sandy Hook.

Return to Lincroft via Rumson and Red Bank over more straight, tree-lined, wide, gently rolling roads. You might wish to view a coastal swamp on nature trails at Fair Haven Fields.

Directions to Starting Point: Thompson Park is on Route 520, two miles west of Garden State Parkway Exit 109, on the left. Note that there is also a Middletown Township park called Thompson Park. You are looking for the Monmouth County facility of the same name. Park near the rose garden. The cue sheet begins at the park exit on Route 520.

Pt.-Pt.	Cume	Turn	Street/Landmark
0.0	0.0	**L**	At exit of Thompson Park onto **Rt. 520 West**
0.4	0.4	**R**	**Greentree Ter.**
0.4	0.8	**R**	**Crawfords Corner-Everett Rd.** (T; no street sign)
0.4	1.2	**R**	**West Front St.**
1.1	2.3	**S**	Cross County Rt. 50/Middletown-Lincroft Rd. at traffic light
0.8	3.1	**S**	Cross Normandy Rd. at traffic light
1.5	4.6		**Deli** on right. Caution on narrow, grated bridge after the deli
0.6	5.2		Road becomes **County Rt. 10/Front St.** in downtown **Red Bank**. Antique stores on either side of street
0.5	5.7		Side-trip to **park overlooking Navesink River**— turn **left** at **Wharf Ave.** then return to **Front St.** and turn **left.** Front St. will eventually change name to **River Rd.**
3.4	9.1	**L**	**Bingham Ave./County Rt. 8-A.** Sign for Oceanic Bridge/Locust
0.9	10.0	**R**	At T, to continue on **Rt. 8-A**
0.5	10.5	**S**	Onto **Locust Point Rd.** Locust Ave./Rt. 8-A goes right
0.9	11.4	**S**	At stop sign, onto **Navesink Ave. General Store** on right, closed Sunday
0.4	11.8	**S**	Cross Rt. 36 at traffic light. Road has changed name to **Grand Ave.**
0.4	12.2	**R**	**Highland Ave.** Turn is just before underpass
0.6	12.8	**S**	At stop sign onto unmarked **Ocean Blvd.**
0.2	13.0	**L**	**Prospect Rd.** This is a narrow road and easy to miss. *CAUTION:* Control your speed on steep, winding downhill!
0.3	13.3	**R**	**Bayside Dr.** (T)
1.3	14.6	**R**	**Shore Dr.** (T; no street sign)
0.2	14.8	**L**	**Water Witch Ave.** (stop sign; no street sign)
0.1	14.9	**R**	**Bay Ave./County Rt. 8** (stop sign)
0.9	15.8	**R**	After underpass, toward Sea Bright and Long Branch
0.1	15.9	**S**	**Highland Ave.**
0.1	16.0	**BL**	Toward Twin Lights onto narrow road up very steep hill
0.2	16.2		**Twin Lights museum**, lunch spot. After stopping at lighthouse, return the way you came, controlling your speed on the downhill

Pt.-Pt.	Cume	Turn	Street/Landmark
0.2	16.4	**BR**	At bottom of hill
0.1	16.5	**L**	**Portland Rd.** (stop sign)
0.0	16.5	**R**	**Rt. 36** (cross drawbridge)
0.4	16.9	**BR**	Onto **ramp** toward Sandy Hook (cyclists enter free; ride to the right of the toll booths)
2.4	19.3		**Spermacetti Cove Visitor's Center** on right
1.4	20.7	**R**	Toward Gunnison Beach and North Beach (street is called **Atlantic Ave.**)
1.3	22.0		**Gunnison Beach** (entrance on right; restrooms and water fountain available). Then continue cycling north, toward North Beach and Fort Hancock
0.1	22.1	**R**	**Atlantic Dr.**
0.7	22.8	**SL**	Turn sharp left where fenced-in restricted area is straight ahead
0.1	22.9	**R**	**Canfield Rd.** (T; no sign)
0.1	23.0	**L**	**Hartshorne Dr.** (unmarked). **Coast Guard station** is straight ahead before you make this turn
0.4	23.4		**History House** on left
0.1	23.5	**L**	**Hudson Rd.**
0.1	23.6		**Sandy Hook Museum** on left
0.1	23.7		**Lighthouse** on left (building not open to public). Interesting old batteries (forts) behind lighthouse. Route turns right here
0.4	24.1	**BL**	Past rockets on pedestals onto road paralleling Raritan Bay
0.2	24.3		Hiking trail to bayside beach on right
1.8	26.1		**Spermacetti Cove Visitor's Center** on left
3.6	29.7	**BL**	At fork, toward Sea Bright and Long Branch (toward Rt. 36 South)
0.2	29.9	**R**	**Rt. 36 South** (stop sign). *CAUTION:* Watch for double-width bike-killer storm drains extending far out into the road. Very busy traffic in summer!
2.0	31.9	**R**	**Rt. 520 West** (traffic light) toward Rumson. Cross drawbridge
0.3	32.2	**R**	**Ward Ave.** (first right after bridge; may be no sign). Pass white church with red doors on left shortly after turn
0.2	32.4	**L**	**Ridge Rd.** (T; no signs). Road becomes **County Rt. 34**

Pt.-Pt.	Cume	Turn	Street/Landmark
3.1	35.5		**Fair Haven Fields** on right (nature trails). Note that **Ridge Rd.** will change name to **Harding Rd.** and then **Reckless Pl.** as you enter Red Bank
2.1	37.6	R	**Maple Ave.** (T)
0.3	37.9	L	**West Front St.** Keep left at fork immediately past turn, following County Rt. 10
0.4	38.3		Use caution on narrow, grated bridge
1.9	40.2	S	Cross Normandy Rd. at traffic light
0.8	41.0	L	**Middletown-Lincroft Rd./County Rt. 50** (traffic light)
1.1	42.1	R	**Newman Springs Rd./Rt. 520** (traffic light)
0.5	42.6		**Brookdale Community College** on left
0.4	43.0	L	**Thompson Park.** End of route

Howitzer at Fort Hancock

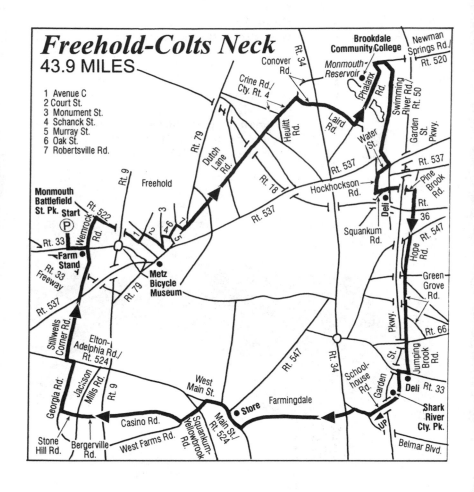

Freehold-Colts Neck
43.9 MILES

1 Avenue C
2 Court St.
3 Monument St.
4 Schanck St.
5 Murray St.
6 Oak St.
7 Robertsville Rd.

Freehold-Colts Neck—43.9 miles

Many thanks to Ira Wiss for suggesting some of the roads used on this route.

Terrain: Hurray! Flat central Jersey. A little rolling at times, and one climb on Schoolhouse Road.

Traffic: Mostly on the light side of moderate. A little heavier on Hope Road east of the Garden State Parkway. Phalanx Road and Route 50 are busy, and Freehold area is also getting busy.

Road Conditions: Good, except around construction zones where homes are being built.

Points of Interest: Monmouth Battlefield State Park (historical exhibits); **Freehold** (pretty county seat community); **Metz Bicycle Museum; Brookdale Community College** (occasional ethnic festivals); **Shark River County Park** (nice lake and picnic spot, mountain biking); **Farmingdale** (another picturesque small village); beautiful riding through Monmouth County woods and horse country.

Colts Neck is appropriately named. You'll see lots of colts here, as well as horses of all types. This part of Monmouth County is truly a home for New Jersey's state animal.

Start by heading east out of Monmouth Battlefield to Freehold. This is a picturesque town with a grand park in front of the large old courthouse, pretty homes on quiet tree-lined streets and the feeling of time standing still.

Take a slight detour off the main route if you wish to visit the Metz Bicycle Museum. This facility, a labor of love by a 50-year collector of all types of human-powered antiques, is located at 54 West Main Street in Freehold and is open Wednesdays and Saturdays from 12:30 to 4:30 p.m. or by appointment. Admission is $5. Telephone (732) 462-7363 for more information.

Next head up through the horsey country of Colts Neck. You'll be on Dutch Lane for a number of miles—this road was quite rural ten years ago but is suburbanizing fast.

Head for Brookdale Community College. There are occasional ethnic festivals here, including a Celtic Festival in mid-September, worth stopping for.

Head south on Swimming River Road and enter a pretty area near Fort Monmouth (Water Street and Hockhockson Road). Buy a snack at the deli, then ride south parallel to the Garden State Parkway. A good place to stop for lunch is Shark River County Park, which has a pretty lake rimmed with pine trees. Some off-road riding is available here.

Soon you'll be in Farmingdale and the flat farm country surrounding it. Casino Road is particularly pretty. Be sure to patronize the farm stand near Monmouth Battlefield, which makes its own cider from apples grown adjacent to the stand.

Directions to Starting Point: Monmouth Battlefield State Park is off Business Route 33, about 2 miles west of Route 9 and 10 miles east of New Jersey Turnpike Exit 8. Park at any picnic ground. The cue sheet starts at the first intersection in the park.

Pt.-Pt.	Cume	Turn	Street/Landmark
0.0	0.0		From the first intersection in **Monmouth Battlefield State Park**, ride down the hill toward the park exit
0.4	0.4	L	**Business Rt. 33 East** (T)
0.2	0.6	L	**Wemrock Rd.** (traffic light)
1.1	1.7	R	**Rt. 522** (T)
0.6	2.3		Ride under Rt. 9
0.6	2.9	L	**Avenue C**. To visit **Metz Bicycle Museum**, continue **straight** here instead for 0.3 miles to where road ends at West Main St. Cross street to enter museum, located in an old car dealership. After visiting the museum, cycle to the **right** on **Main St. Bear left** at the fork, following **Broadway/Rt. 79 North**. Rejoin the route at Mile 4.2.
0.2	3.1	R	**Court St.** (stop sign)
0.3	3.4	SL	**Monument St.**
0.1	3.5	R	**Schanck St.**
0.2	3.7	BL	Onto **Oak St.** Murray St. goes right
0.3	4.0	R	**Robertsville Rd.** (T)
0.1	4.1	L	**Broadway/Rt. 79 North** (T)
0.1	4.2	BR	**Dutch Lane Rd./County Rt. 46**
5.0	9.2	S	Onto **County Rt. 4** (unmarked **Crine Rd.**) at intersection of Heulitt Rd.
0.7	9.9	R	**Conover Rd.** (T)
0.5	10.4	S	Cross Rt. 34 at stop sign onto **Laird Rd.**
2.1	12.5	L	**Phalanx Rd.** (stop sign)
1.6	14.1		**Brookdale Community College** (festivals) on left
0.4	14.5	R	**Newman Springs Rd./Rt. 520** (traffic light)

Pt.-Pt.	Cume	Turn	Street/Landmark
0.1	14.6	R	**Swimming River Rd./County Rt. 50**
1.2	15.8	S	At traffic light, crossing the government road and railroad tracks
0.7	16.5	L	**Rt. 537 East** (traffic light)
0.4	16.9	R	**Water St.** (traffic light; Portofino Restaurant on corner)
1.4	18.3	L	**Hockhockson Rd.** (T)
0.7	19.0		Park on left. Good picnic spot
0.2	19.2	L	**Squankum Rd.** (T)
0.3	19.5		**Deli** on right (closed Sunday). Then **straight** at the traffic light. Road becomes **Pine Brook Rd.**
1.0	20.5	R	**Hope Rd.** (traffic light). Continue **straight** through all stop signs and traffic lights. Road will eventually change name to **Green Grove Rd.**
4.3	24.8	BR	At fork onto **Jumping Brook Rd.** Green Grove Rd. goes left
0.9	25.7	S	Cross Rt. 66 at traffic light
1.0	26.7	R	**Rt. 33** (traffic light). **Deli** across highway
0.3	27.0	L	**Schoolhouse Rd.** (traffic light)
0.4	27.4		**Shark River County Park.** Nice lake on right for picnics
1.0	28.4	R	**Belmar Blvd./County Rt. 18** (T)
0.7	29.1	S	Cross Rt. 34
2.5	31.6	R	**Main St./Rt. 524 West** (T)
0.2	31.8		**Store** on right
0.4	32.2	L	Curve left onto **West Main St.**
0.7	32.9	L	**West Farms Rd.**
0.4	33.3	S	Cross Squankum-Yellowbrook Rd. at stop sign
0.7	34.0	R	**Casino Rd.**
3.2	37.2	S	Cross Rt. 9 at traffic light. Road becomes **Bergerville Rd.**
1.3	38.5	S	Cross Jackson Mills Rd. at stop sign. Road you are on will change name to **Stone Hill Rd.**
0.9	39.4	R	**Georgia Rd.** (T)
0.8	40.2	L	**Elton-Adelphia Rd./Rt. 524** (T)
0.1	40.3	R	**Stillwells Corner Rd.** (busy road)
1.7	42.0	S	Cross Rt. 537 at traffic light. Road becomes **Wemrock Rd.**
0.8	42.8		Cross over Rt. 33 freeway
0.5	43.3	L	**Business Rt. 33 West** (traffic light). Farm stand on corner
0.2	43.5	R	Into **Monmouth Battlefield State Park**
0.4	43.9		First intersection in park. End of route

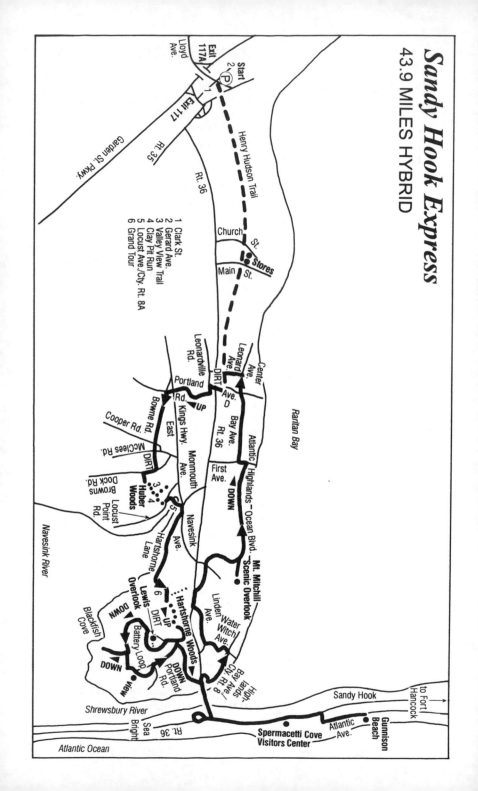

Sandy Hook Express—43.9 miles
(Hybrid)

The Henry Hudson Trail, a nine-mile bike path paralleling Route 36, makes it possible to ride to Sandy Hook in a hurry. Since this path used to be a railroad right-of-way, the name Sandy Hook Express is fitting for this route.

Terrain: Flat on the bike path. Very hilly in the Highlands/Atlantic Highlands region as you approach and leave Sandy Hook. The hills in Hartshorne Woods are especially steep. Sandy Hook itself is flat, but often windy.

Traffic: No cars on the bike path and on the couple of mountain bike "samplers" in Huber and Hartshorne Woods. Traffic light to moderate otherwise. This is probably the most car-free bike approach to Sandy Hook.

Road Conditions: Henry Hudson Trail is well maintained, as are the roads in the communities of Navesink, Highlands, Atlantic Highlands and Middletown. Mountain bike trails in Huber Woods and Hartshorne Woods are of moderate difficulty.

Points of Interest: Views of **coastal wetlands** and **inlets** along the Henry Hudson Trail; excellent woodland trails in **Huber Woods** and **Hartshorne Woods**; view of river and ocean from **World War II bunker** and several places near and in Hartshorne Woods; **Sandy Hook** swimming; return via scenic route and **Mount Mitchill**.

This new *RIDE GUIDE* route presents a third alternative for cyclists to reach Sandy Hook, and is one of our favorites. Riders can start pedaling minutes off the Garden State Parkway and ride nine miles car-free along a paved rail-trail path.

The Henry Hudson Trail, maintained by the Monmouth County Park Commission, is very scenic considering it used to be a railroad spur serving industry along Raritan Bay. Besides passing the backyards of modest suburban homes and newer condominium developments (and the backs of occasional factories), the path features several incredible views of tidal wetlands and estuaries. Watch for butterflies, shore and land birds, and perhaps even a turtle or two. None of these views are visible driving on Route 36 to Sandy Hook.

Henry Hudson Trail crosses local streets many, many times. I only mention the most prominent street crossings in the cue sheet. Each crossing deserves a stop and look for cars, as foliage often obscures the view. Another caution for cyclists is the many wooden-floored bridges. These are a little bumpy, and get slippery when wet.

The paved path ends nine miles from its Aberdeen start in the town of Leonardo. It continues for a half-mile or so as a dirt path. A road alternative is described.

Flatness now comes to an end. Unlike other New Jersey Shore areas, the Highlands are hilly, as the name implies. Climb Portland Road, adjacent to the Beacon Hill Country Club. Then cycle through some fine horse country, with lots of large hardwood and evergreen trees to shade you. The terrain and look of this area is similar to the horse country of Hunterdon County.

A paved alternate cutting 4.5 miles off the total distance is described in the cue sheet, and zips riders right to Sandy Hook. For those with hybrid bikes or all-terrain bikes, stay with the dirt road. Soon you will be in Huber Woods, one of two fine Monmouth County parks in the Highlands area that feature excellent mountain biking trails.

This route provides a sampler of Huber Woods trails. The Valley View Trail is a wonderful, easy, all-downhill hardpacked singletrack through beautiful rhododendron groves. Watch out for deer! Also look out for the odd stump that sticks up into the trail.

Clay Pit Run, which takes the cyclist east out of Huber Woods and toward Hartshorne Woods, is a more advanced trail. You may have to walk several of the steep hills; they have suffered much erosion and there are a number of sandy spots that will stop you dead in your tracks.

You will emerge on somewhat busy roads that take you over a bridge over an inlet of the Navesink River. Next, turn on a dead-end road with almost no traffic that passes a number of riverside estates. A downhill charge and you are cycling on a causeway featuring a picture-perfect view of the Navesink.

Near the dead-end are two entrances to Hartshorne Woods Park open only to walkers and cyclists. The path with the wooden gate leads to some of the difficult runs that make this park famous for ATBers seeking a challenge. The dirt road with the metal gate is the one this route follows, because it leads directly (and all up hill, alas) to the former Army area that is one of the highlights of this tour.

After reaching the Portland Road entrance to the park, head toward the manmade mound. This is a World War II bunker used to house guns which protected the Atlantic Coast. In the 1950s the area was a missile control center. Since the 1980s this has been part of Hartshorne Woods.

A skinny singletrack climbs the mound. Enjoy the fabulous view of the Navesink River, the Shrewsbury River, the tiny spit of land that is Sea Bright, and the ocean beyond. Then descend and pedal the loop of paved roads that comes down from the high point to the shore of the Navesink by Blackfish Cove, an excellent picnic spot.

Climb back up for a few more views, then charge downhill out of the park, over the drawbridge and onto Sandy Hook for a well-deserved swim. Note that this route goes to Gunnison Beach, famous for its "clothing-optional" section. Any protected beach along the Hook is excellent for swimming. Those wishing to cut a few miles would have just as good a time at the very first beach, about half a mile from the toll booth (bikes enter free, by the way).

The return route is far less extreme as far as hills go. Ride along Raritan Bay through the Highlands, which features all manner of seafood restaurants. Climb back to Route 36, then just one more climb: to Mount Mitchill, with an extraordinary view encompassing all of Sandy Hook, Raritan Bay, and up to the narrows, the Verrazano Bridge, and the towers of Manhattan.

Your climbing is over! It's downhill along curvy, scenic Ocean Boulevard (the "scenic route"), all the way to Atlantic Highlands. Then a relatively flat spin through quiet residential streets until you re-enter the Henry Hudson Trail for the nine-mile, traffic-free pedal back to your car.

Directions to Starting Point: The route starts across from the **western terminus of the Henry Hudson Trail**. From the north, take Garden State Parkway to Exit 117A-Aberdeen (be sure to stay to the right after the Raritan Tolls and take the local lanes; also be sure to have a quarter, as frequently they have only a gated exact-change lane open and no manned tollbooth). Turn left at the traffic light at the top of the ramp. Pass the first light, corner of Lloyd and Gerard Avenue, and immediately turn left into a parking lot by a baseball field that is across the street from a Shell gas station.

From the south, take Exit 117 of the Garden State Parkway northbound local lanes. Follow signs for Route 35. Immediately get in the left lane and U-turn onto Route 35 north. Stay left again and exit as if going back on the Parkway. Then turn right immediately before the tolls onto Clark Street. Drive to the first traffic light, which is Lloyd Avenue, turn right, then immediately turn left into a parking lot by a baseball field that is across the street from a Shell gas station.

Pt.-Pt.	Cume	Turn	Street/Landmark
0.0	0.0		Cross the street to the Shell Station and start the **Henry Hudson Trail** by riding next to the guardrail, then turning **right** onto the trail
1.1	1.1		At Cornucopia Restaurant, cross wide road, head for Atlantic Street, and then turn **right** to continue on trail
1.5	2.6		Bike path goes between a school and a ballfield. Shady part ends for quite awhile
0.6	3.2		Excellent view of tidal wetlands on left with view of **Raritan Bay** and **Verrazano Narrows Bridge**
0.7	3.9		Cross a tidal estuary. First sighting of boats that can get to the bay and ocean (on the left)
0.6	4.5		Cross Church St. Busy road, limited visibility as road curves right at the path crossing. **Store** on left (note bear sculptures behind store)
0.2	4.7		Cross Main St. Busy road, another **food store** available on left
4.2	8.9		Paved path ends at Leonard Ave. Continue **straight on dirt path** (*for all-paved route:* turn **right on Leonard Ave.**, cross Rt. 36 at the traffic light, then make the next **left onto Leonardville Rd.** Proceed 0.4 miles to **Portland Rd.** and turn **right**, which is the turn at mile 9.6)
0.4	9.3		Dirt path emerges at parking lot. Ride through, behind a restaurant and fruit stand. Continue on bumpy dirt road
0.1	9.4	**R**	Path ends at **Avenue D**. Turn right
0.1	9.5	**S**	Cross Rt. 36 at traffic light
0.1	9.6	**L**	At stop sign
0.0	9.6	**R**	Immediate right onto **Portland Rd.** (Beacon Hill Country Club on right). Climb, gently and steady at first then steeper and steeper

Pt.-Pt.	Cume	Turn	Street/Landmark
0.8	10.4		Top of hill. Hurray!
1.0	11.4	**S**	At stop sign, cross Kings Highway East to continue on **Portland Rd.** (*all-paved route:* **turn left** here. The road becomes **Monmouth Ave.** In 1.5 miles, **bear right onto Navesink Ave./ County Rt. 8-B**. Ride 1 mile to **Route 36, turn right** (east) and follow Rt. 36 1.3 miles. If you wish to pedal up hill to see the bunker area of Hartshorne Woods park and the view of the Navesink River at Blackfish Cove, **turn right** at **Portland Rd.** immediately before the drawbridge and ride 0.8 miles. Rejoin the main route at mile 17.3. Otherwise cross the drawbridge to Sandy Hook and rejoin the main route at mile 20.7)
0.1	11.5	**L**	**Bowne Rd.** (straight ahead is dirt and downhill)
0.5	12.0	**S**	At stop sign. Cooper Road goes right
0.1	12.1	**S**	At stop sign. Cross McClees Rd. **Bowne Road becomes dirt**
0.5	12.6	**R**	At unmarked dirt T onto **Browns Dock Rd.**, where left turn goes down hill. You climb
0.1	12.7	**L**	**Huber Woods parking lot** (paved)
0.1	12.8		Huber Woods buildings. Excellent restroom and water stop. Note great view of **Navesink River**. Then, opposite parking lot from buildings, ride the **narrow dirt path** across a wide meadow and enter the woods.
0.0	12.8	**R**	At trail junction by bulletin board with trail map onto the (unmarked) **Valley View Trail**. Do not go onto nature trail
0.3	13.1	**R**	At fork, following **blue square trail**
0.2	13.3	**R**	**Clay Pit Run trail.** *CAUTION:* Many difficult spots that are sandy, steep, eroded and full of roots. Walk where necessary
0.5	13.8	**R**	Emerge from woods onto **wide gravel road**. Turn right toward houses outside the park
0.1	13.9	**L**	Onto **busy paved road**
0.1	14.0	**R**	**Locust Ave./County Rt. 8-A.** Cross bridge over inlet. Use wooden sidewalk rather than grated road surface. Then climb

Pt.-Pt.	Cume	Turn	Street/Landmark
0.4	14.4	**R**	At Y intersection onto **Navesink Ave./County Rt. 8-B**
0.1	14.5	**R**	**Hartshorne Lane** (a dead-end road)
1.0	15.5		Downhill begins. Glorious view of river inlet ahead. One of prettiest on Jersey Shore. Get your cameras ready! Shortly after, road changes name to **Grand Tour**
0.7	16.2		Entrance to **Hartshorne Woods** mountain biking paths on left (wooden gate with sign saying "no parking")
0.2	16.4	**L**	At metal gate onto **hard-packed gravel road** marked with a sign "Park system vehicles only". Steep climb
0.3	16.7	**L**	Onto **paved path**
0.2	16.9	**R**	Emerge at **Portland Road parking area**. Turn right toward the obvious bunkers
0.1	17.0	**L**	Turn left, following signs for Lewis Overlook. Trail goes under **Battery Lewis bunker** (1942)
0.1	17.1	**R**	Immediate right after the underpass on singletrack which climbs the bunker. **Bear left** at the fork to circle on top of the bunker. Enjoy a tremendous view of **Sea Bright**, the **Shrewsbury River** (intercoastal waterway) and the **Atlantic Ocean** at one of the switchbacks. Then circle around and make a **sharp left** to go back down the way you came up
0.2	17.3	**R**	Right at end of singletrack onto **paved road** circling around bunkers. Continue **straight** past the next possible underpass under the bunker
0.2	17.5	**L**	Turn left past end of bunker onto **wide paved road (the Battery Loop)**, curving around and downhill. Follow the widest paved road at all intersections
0.5	18.0	**R**	At the bottom of a tremendous hill, turn right to head toward **Blackfish Cove**. You will go down another hill
0.1	18.1	**L**	Take the left loop as you enter a small picnic area, and continue down the road to the banks of the **Navesink River**. Great photo spot! Turn around and climb back up (huff-puff, huff-puff!)

Pt.-Pt.	Cume	Turn	Street/Landmark
0.3	18.4	**R**	Turn right at the top of the hill (T) to resume the **Battery Loop**
0.1	18.5	**R**	Turn right at the next fork as you approach the next bunkers. You will enjoy another great view of ocean and river
0.5	19.0	**R**	Turn right to exit park onto **Portland Rd.**
0.1	19.1	**S**	At stop sign. Enough uphill! (which is what you would face if you turned left here). Go straight, down the hill, and watch your speed! Enjoy river, ocean views, and large homes
0.8	19.9	**S**	Cross Highland Ave. (turn **left** and prepare to climb again if you wish to visit **Twin Lights State Historic Site**)
0.0	19.9	**R**	**Rt. 36.** Cross drawbridge toward Sandy Hook
0.4	20.3	**BR**	Onto **ramp** toward Sandy Hook (you may ride through toll booths; cyclists enter free)
2.4	22.7		Spermacetti Cove Visitor's Center on right
1.4	24.1	**R**	Toward Gunnison Beach and North Beach (street is called **Atlantic Ave.**)
1.3	25.4		**Gunnison Beach** (entrance on right; bathrooms and water fountain available). Then cycle back in the direction you came from
1.2	26.6	**L**	At T toward park exit. (If you wish to tour **Fort Hancock**, turn **right** here)
3.6	30.2	**BR**	At fork onto **Rt. 36 West** (cross drawbridge)
0.3	30.5	**R**	Toward Highlands business center
0.1	30.6	**L**	At bottom of hill onto **County Rt. 8**
0.9	31.5	**L**	**Water Witch Ave./County Rt. 8.** Climb a hill
0.2	31.7	**R**	**Linden Ave./County Rt. 8.** Continue climbing
0.3	32.0	**R**	At traffic light onto **Rt. 36.**
0.1	32.1	**R**	Jug handle marked Red Bank/Scenic Road
0.1	32.2	**S**	Stop sign, toward Scenic Road and Mount Mitchill
0.2	32.4	**R**	Toward Mount Mitchill. Enjoy view, then return to stop sign
0.1	32.5	**BR**	**Ocean Blvd.** Get ready for long, curvy downhill
1.1	33.6	**L**	**First Ave.**, Atlantic Highlands (T)
0.1	33.7	**R**	Immediate right onto **Bay Ave.**
0.2	33.9	**L**	**Avenue D** (T)

Pt.-Pt.	Cume	Turn	Street/Landmark
0.1	34.0	R	**Center Ave.** (Stop sign)
0.6	34.6	L	**Leonard Ave.**
0.3	34.9	R	**Henry Hudson Trail** bike path (right before Rt. 36 traffic light)
9.0	43.9		Cross Lloyd Ave. End of route

Officer's Row at Fort Hancock

Cheesequake-Sandy Hook—61.4 miles

This route originally appeared in RIDE GUIDE For North Jersey and Beyond. *It's still one of the best and most challenging ways to get to the northernmost outpost of the Jersey Shore.*

Terrain: Rolling, since this is the Highlands, the hilly part of the shore. The steeper stretches occur on Navesink River Road and Kings Highway.

Traffic: Light to moderate near the beginning, then moderate thereafter. A short stretch on a busy highway approaching Sandy Hook (wide shoulder available).

Road Conditions: Good. All paved roads, very little choppy pavement.

Points of Interest: Twin Lights State Historic Site; Sandy Hook unit of **Gateway National Park** (swimming and beach-walking); views of bay, ocean, and **New York Skyline** from Mt. Mitchill and Ocean Blvd.; quiet and pretty Monmouth County **horse country** back roads.

This challenging route is an ideal way to increase your maximum distance—as many cyclists have done with it over the years. The reward of a cool dip in the ocean has a way of bringing out additional miles from tired legs.

Beautiful scenery, both inland and shoreside, make this ride even more enjoyable. The serenity of the roads is especially remarkable considering you begin not far from the busy Garden State Parkway.

Head through a small corner of Old Bridge, Middlesex County before entering Monmouth County. Marlboro and Holmdel townships still have many working farms and are full of pleasant vistas and lightly rolling terrain. A store just past the 15-mile point is well equipped to provide a snack or a picnic lunch for eating later at the lighthouse or beach.

Soon you'll be on Navesink River Road. The hills get more demanding here as you head by large riverfront estates. Views of sailboats, shore birds and the smell of the sea start taking on prominence—the ocean is near.

Topping a rise on Route 36, the ocean is visible at last. But don't cross the drawbridge just yet. Instead, climb the hill to Twin Lights State

Historic Site. There is a fascinating museum here depicting lifesaving devices used to rescue shipwrecked passengers in the 19th-century. You can climb to the top of one of the lighthouse towers and enjoy a panoramic view, and then have lunch on the grass below. A separate building houses the old light and the lens that magnified the light so well that it could be seen 50 miles out to sea. Restrooms and cold water are available in the museum building.

Next, head out to Sandy Hook. You are almost guaranteed a strong headwind, tailwind, or crosswind while cycling on the Hook, which is a thin peninsula between the ocean and Raritan Bay. Besides stopping for a swim at Gunnison Beach, you might wish to explore the Spermacetti Cove Visitor's Center, which has many interesting exhibits on marine life, or perhaps tour Fort Hancock. There are many old buildings on the Hook that date from the time when this was an important military base and munitions testing center.

Take note that Gunnison Beach is well-known as one of the largest "natural" beaches on the East Coast. "Natural," as in bathing-suit optional. If this does not appeal to you, there are countless other beaches on Sandy Hook where you can swim.

Return to the "mainland" via the drawbridge. Enjoy your last views of bay and ocean from the Mt. Mitchill scenic overlook and while zooming down Ocean Boulevard. The return route is through rolling country past horse farms and quiet towns such as Middletown and Matawan. A swimming beach awaits you at Cheesequake State Park.

Directions to Starting Point: Cheesequake State Park is located off of Garden State Parkway Exit 120. Turn right at the top of the ramp. Make a right turn at the first traffic light onto Cliffwood Road, then turn right at the next traffic light onto Gordon Road. Follow the signs to the park entrance, then follow the signs to the lake beach parking area.

Pt.-Pt.	Cume	Turn	Street/Landmark
0.0	0.0		Exit lake parking area the way you drove in
0.2	0.2	R	Toward park exit
0.1	0.3	R	Toward park exit
0.2	0.5	R	Toward park exit, and out of park
1.1	1.6	R	At traffic light onto **Morristown Rd.**
0.4	2.0	L	**Disbrow Rd.**
0.3	2.3	S	Cross Rt. 34 at traffic light
0.4	2.7	L	**Browns Rd.** (T; no street sign)

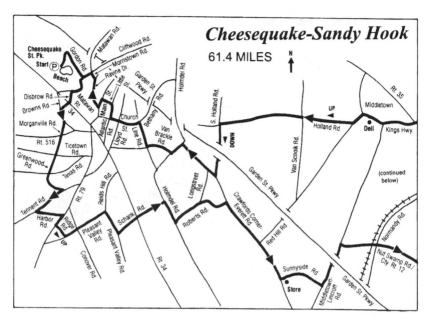

Cheesequake-Sandy Hook

61.4 MILES

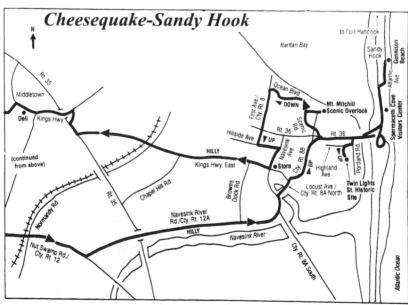

Cheesequake-Sandy Hook

Pt.-Pt.	Cume	Turn	Street/Landmark
0.6	3.3	R	**Morganville Rd.**
0.2	3.5	S	At stop sign, crossing unmarked Rt. 516
1.2	4.7	S	Cross Ticetown Rd. Road you are on has changed name to **Greenwood Rd.**
0.4	5.1	S	Cross Texas Rd.
0.6	5.7	R	**Tennent Rd.** (T)
1.3	7.0	L	**Harbor Rd.**
1.2	8.2	R	**Rt. 79** (T; no street sign)
0.2	8.4	L	**Ridge Rd.**
0.4	8.8	L	**Pleasant Valley Rd.** (T; no street sign)
0.8	9.6	S	Cross Conover Rd. at stop sign
1.3	10.9	R	At T, to continue on **Pleasant Valley Rd.** (Reids Hill Rd. goes left)
0.8	11.7	L	**Schank Rd.**
0.8	12.5	S	Cross Rt. 34 at stop sign
0.4	12.9	R	**Holmdel Rd.** (T)
0.2	13.1	L	**Roberts Rd.**
0.6	13.7	R	At curve to continue on **Roberts Rd.** (Longstreet Rd. goes left)
0.8	14.5	R	**Crawfords Corner-Everett Rd.** (T; no street sign)
2.1	16.6	L	**Sunnyside Rd.** (**store** on right after making turn)
1.2	17.8	L	**Middletown-Lincroft Rd.** (T). You will go under Garden State Pkwy. shortly after making turn)
1.0	18.8	R	**Nut Swamp Rd./County Rt. 12** (traffic light)
0.5	19.3	S	At traffic light by railroad crossing
1.4	20.7	L	**Navesink River Rd./County Rt. 12-A**
0.6	21.3	S	Cross Rt. 35 at traffic light
3.9	25.2	S	Onto **County Rt. 8-A North** (Rt. 8-A South turns right)
0.5	25.7	R	**Locust Ave./Rt. 8-A North** (cross bridge over tidal inlet immediately)
0.4	26.1	R	**Rt. 8-B** (toward Highlands and Rt. 36 East; **curve left** immediately after turn, heading uphill toward Gateway National Park)
1.0	27.1	BR	**Rt. 36 East** (toward Highlands)
1.3	28.4	R	Toward Twin Lights State Historic Site (turn is immediately before drawbridge)
0.0	28.4	R	Immediate right onto **Highland Ave.**
0.1	28.5	BL	Toward Twin Lights onto narrow road up very steep hill

Pt.-Pt.	Cume	Turn	Street/Landmark
0.2	28.7		**Twin Lights museum**, lunch spot. After stopping at lighthouse, return the way you came, controlling your speed on the downhill
0.2	28.9	**BR**	At bottom of hill
0.1	29.0	**L**	**Portland Rd.** (stop sign)
0.0	29.0	**R**	**Rt. 36** (cross drawbridge)
0.4	29.4	**BR**	Onto **ramp** toward Sandy Hook (you may ride through the toll booths; cyclists enter free)
2.4	31.8		**Spermacetti Cove Visitor's Center** on right
1.4	33.2	**R**	Toward Gunnison Beach and North Beach (street is called **Atlantic Ave.**)
1.3	34.5		**Gunnison Beach** (entrance on right; bathrooms and water fountain available). Then cycle back in the direction you came from
1.2	35.7	**L**	At T toward park exit. (If you wish to tour **Fort Hancock, turn right** here)
3.6	39.3	**BR**	At fork onto **Rt. 36 West** (cross drawbridge)
1.6	40.9	**BR**	At jughandle for Red Bank/Scenic Rd.
0.1	41.0	**S**	At stop sign at top of jughandle, toward Scenic Rd.
0.2	41.2	**R**	Into **Mt. Mitchill Scenic Overlook**; then U-turn and go straight onto **Ocean Blvd.**
1.0	42.2	**R**	At sharp curve to continue on **Ocean Blvd.** Control your speed on this curvy, steep downhill!
1.1	43.3	**L**	**First Ave./County Rt. 8**
0.4	43.7	**S**	Cross Rt. 36 at traffic light
0.4	44.1	**L**	**Hillside Ave.** (T)
0.5	44.6	**R**	**Navesink Ave.** (T)
0.1	44.7	**R**	**Kings Highway East** (stop sign; no street sign). **Store** on left at corner
2.9	47.6	**S**	Cross Normandy Rd. and railroad tracks at traffic light
0.9	48.5	**R**	**Rt. 35 North** (T)
0.0	48.5	**BR**	Immediate **right** into jughandle, then **left** at fork at end of jughandle toward Middletown. Cross Rt. 35 at traffic light onto **Kings Highway**
1.0	49.5		**Deli** on left
0.2	49.7	**L**	**Red Hill Rd.**
0.2	49.9	**R**	**Holland Rd.** (street sign hidden on left)

Pt.-Pt.	Cume	Turn	Street/Landmark
1.4	51.3	S	Cross Van Schoick Rd. at traffic light
0.8	52.1	L	**South Holland Rd.**
0.4	52.5		Ride under Garden State Parkway
0.6	53.1	R	**Crawfords Corner-Everett Rd.** (T)
0.7	53.8	L	**Holmdel Rd.** (T)
0.3	54.1	R	**Van Brackle Rd.**
1.0	55.1	R	**Line Rd.** (stop sign)
1.1	56.2	L	**Church St.** (traffic light; Bethany Rd. goes right)
0.3	56.5	S	Cross Lloyd Rd. at traffic light
0.5	57.0	R	**Atlantic Rd.** (traffic light)
0.5	57.5	L	**Little St.** (turn is just past an overpass and is easy to miss)
0.2	57.7	S	Cross Broad St. (traffic light)
0.1	57.8	L	**Main St.** (T; traffic light; no street sign)
0.1	57.9	R	**Ravine Dr./County Rt. 6-A**
1.4	59.3	L	**Morristown Rd.** Turn is just past "crossed curve sign"
0.2	59.5	L	**Cliffwood Rd.** (traffic light)
0.3	59.8	R	**Gordon Rd.** (traffic light, toward Cheesequake Park)
0.5	60.3	BR	At entrance to apartments, to continue toward park
0.6	60.9	L	At T past park gate toward Hook's Lake
0.2	61.1	L	Toward Lake/Picnic Area
0.1	61.2	L	Toward Lake
0.2	61.4		**Lake**. End of route

Rides Starting in Mercer County

Princeton is the prestige town in New Jersey. The biggest drawing card in the state's real estate market is offices or homes having a Princeton mailing address, even though they may be miles from the University. Despite tremendous growth in the last 10 years in population and office buildings, the Princeton area remains one of the state's hotbeds of bicycle touring. The countryside surrounding the busy college town is still beautiful in all four directions. For that reason, this section consists of four rides, each leaving from Princeton High School, heading off in the major directions of the compass. For train riders with a bike permit, these rides are easily accessible from Princeton Junction station.

Princeton Canalier Ride goes north into Somerset County. After a few initial hills, the terrain settles down to flat or gently rolling as the route shoots up through Montgomery and Hillsborough townships. After a lunch stop at Colonial Park with its beautiful rose garden, the cyclist rides south along the Delaware & Raritan Canal, a tranquil, narrow, tree-lined valley with many interesting old stone buildings and canal locks. The final approach to Princeton is on the old canal towpath, as the cyclist rides along Lake Carnegie and crosses an outlet of the lake along with the canal on an old aqueduct bridge.

Head south from Princeton on the **Princeton-Crosswicks** route. Pass the end of Trenton-Robbinsville Airport's runway before cycling to Crosswicks. This is a 19th-century village with picture-postcard homes and a store/cafe that serves a tasty breakfast and lunch. After riding through gently rolling rural terrain, arrive in Allentown to explore a group of antique stores in an old mill. Flat, quiet, woodsy roads return you to Princeton.

Princeton-Stockton heads west to the Delaware River. En route, you will climb and descend a few steep hills, pass many large horse estates and the pretty old towns of Ringoes and Sergeantsville. See the Green Sergeant's Covered Bridge before enjoying a run down a creek ravine to the Delaware. Then cycle along the river, exploring Stockton, Lambertville, and New Hope, each town containing many photogenic old homes and interesting stores. There are chances to ride on canal towpaths on either side of the river if you wish to avoid cars. Stop by Washington Crossing and see the exhibits portraying the history of the spot where General Washington crossed the Delaware River, then ride back to Princeton over gently rolling terrain.

Princeton-Englishtown is a route long in distance but short on hills. The first stop is Cranbury, a classic small town complete with neat homes and a soda fountain on Main Street. Head east through rural and woodsy terrain to Englishtown, the home of an enormous flea market. Unwind on the way back by spinning fast over flat, straight roads.

The Delaware & Raritan Canal at Stockton

Princeton Canalier Ride—40.8 miles

The Delaware & Raritan Canal is a long linear park extending from New Brunswick to Trenton. The canal's towpath is hard-packed dirt and makes for excellent bike riding, even for skinny-tired bikes. This route features a four-mile section of towpath near the end of the ride, with an option for eight more miles.

Terrain: Some long and rolling hills in the first few miles, otherwise primarily flat.

Traffic: Moderate from Princeton to Hillsborough Road, light after that. No traffic at all along the canal!

Road Conditions: Fair to good pavement at times, much smoother on the return trip. Towpath sections are hard-packed dirt.

Points of Interest: Colonial Park, with its beautiful rose garden; riding alongside the **Delaware & Raritan Canal** (many interesting, old stone buildings, old canal **aqueduct** over Lake Carnegie inlet).

Princeton may be in the midst of the most rapidly developing corridor in New Jersey, but there are still miles of beautiful countryside surrounding it, even to the north, which is the main direction of development.

This ride takes you north through the open spaces of Montgomery and Hillsborough townships in Somerset County, and returns through the more intimate spaces of the Millstone River Valley and the D&R Canal.

Head north along Great Road. Great Road has a number of long ups and downs to warm you up. As you get into Somerset County, the primary direction seems to be down and the panoramas of flat farm country ahead are beautiful.

Route 601 passes several institutions with large plots of land, including North Princeton Developmental Center, Skillman School, and the Carrier Institute. An even larger institution, the Belle Mead General Services Administration warehouse and depot, is on your left as you start heading east to Route 206.

Stock up on food at a diner, the only food stop on the route, then continue east through Hillsborough Township. Cows munch in open fields in view of "marching suburbia"; housing developments are starting to take over farmland.

Cross the Millstone River and D&R Canal and head east and north to Colonial Park. After the one-mile bike path through the park, arrive at the Rudolf Van Der Goot Rose Garden, a good lunch spot. Many wedding parties use the garden as a photo backdrop.

The ride back is flat, pretty, and interesting, following the Millstone River and D&R Canal the entire way. Stop at Blackwells Mills and Griggstown to explore the old stone buildings and locks that are well-preserved reminders of the canal's glory days. This tree-shaded valley is an incredibly tranquil spot in bustling Central Jersey, and a real contrast to the open vistas earlier in the ride.

For three miles ride right on the towpath, a good hard-dirt road with no traffic. The last segment adjoins Lake Carnegie, where Princeton University crew teams practice. Cross the lake's outlet with the canal on an aqueduct bridge, one of the most beautiful and interesting spots on the whole canal. Return to Princeton on Harrison Street, passing some large old homes.

Directions to Starting Point: Princeton High School is several blocks from the Princeton business district. From U.S. 1, exit at Washington Road/Princeton/Hightstown/Routes 526 and 571. Follow Washington Road into Princeton. Cross Nassau Street/Route 27 just past the University (1.5 miles from Route 1). You will be on Vandeventer Avenue. Turn right at the stop sign onto Wiggins Street, then turn left in several blocks onto Moore Street. A right on Houghton Road as you reach the high school brings you to a parking lot (on the left), where the ride begins.

Train riders: From Princeton Junction's southbound platform, ride through the parking lot and out to Washington Road. Pedal 3 miles to Nassau Street in Princeton then follow the car directions onto Vandeventer Avenue and on to the starting point.

Upon return, you can continue on the D&R Canal towpath past Harrison Street (Mile 38.7) to Washington Road, which is the next road crossing. Turn left and ride to Princeton Junction station.

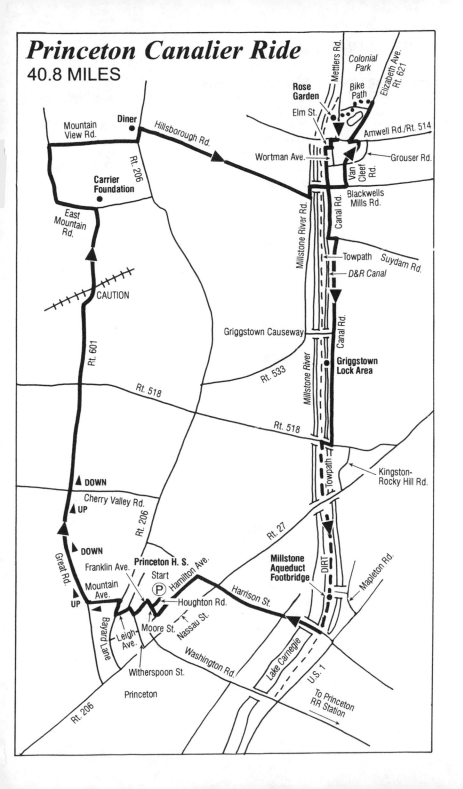

Pt.-Pt.	Cume	Turn	Street/Landmark
0.0	0.0	**R**	Exit high school parking lot and turn right on **Houghton Rd.**
0.1	0.1	**R**	**Moore St.** (T)
0.1	0.2	**L**	**Franklin Ave.**
0.2	0.4	**R**	**Witherspoon St.** (T)
0.1	0.5	**L**	**Leigh Ave.**
0.4	0.9	**R**	**Bayard Lane** (T)
0.1	1.0	**BR**	Into jughandle marked Mountain Ave./Bayard Lane. Go straight at traffic light onto **Mountain Ave.**
0.7	1.7	**R**	**Great Rd.** (T)
2.2	3.9	**S**	Cross Cherry Valley Rd. at stop sign
1.9	5.8	**S**	Cross Rt. 518 at traffic light. Road you are on is **Rt. 601**
2.0	7.8		Watch for railroad crossing; tracks cross road at a dangerous angle
2.2	10.0	**L**	**East Mountain Rd.** If you pass the Carrier Foundation, you've gone too far
2.0	12.0	**R**	**Mountain View Rd.** (street sign is on the left)
2.2	14.2	**L**	**Rt. 206** (T). **Diner** on the left shortly after the turn. This is the only food stop on the route
0.3	14.5	**R**	**Hillsborough Rd.**
4.1	18.6	**L**	**Millstone River Rd.** (T)
0.6	19.2	**R**	**Blackwells Mills Rd.**
0.9	20.1	**L**	**Van Cleef Rd.** Turn is at the top of the hill. A double curve/35 mph sign is straight ahead on Blackwells Mills Rd. after the turn. Ride through new suburbia, soon passing an operational windmill that was retained from when this was a farm
1.5	21.6	**L**	**Amwell Rd./Rt. 514** (T; no street sign)
0.3	21.9	**R**	**Elizabeth Ave./Rt. 621 North** (traffic light)
0.7	22.6	**L**	**Colonial Park Bike Path** (just past road entrance to Colonial Park)
0.9	23.5		Bike path crosses road by pond
0.4	23.9	**L**	**Mettlers Rd.** (next road crossing; no sign)
0.1	24.0	**R**	Toward Arboretum/Rose Garden
0.1	24.1		**Rudolf W. Van Der Goot Rose Garden**. Open 10 a.m. to 8 p.m. Memorial Day through Labor Day; and until 4:30 p.m. Labor Day until Oct. 31. After viewing rose garden, cycle back the way you came in

Pt.-Pt.	Cume	Turn	Street/Landmark
0.1	24.2	R	**Mettlers Rd.** (T)
0.4	24.6	R	**Amwell Rd./Rt. 514** (T)
0.2	24.8	L	**Wortman Ave.**
0.3	25.1	R	**Elm St.**
0.2	25.3	L	Curve left onto **Canal Rd.** (may be no street sign). Road parallels Delaware & Raritan Canal
2.0	27.3	S	Cross Blackwells Mills Rd. at stop sign. You may turn right here, cross the canal and enter the towpath if you prefer
1.3	28.6	R	To continue on **Canal Rd.** Suydam Rd. goes straight. Water treatment plant on right at turn
2.3	30.9		**Griggstown Causeway** on right—interesting old stone canal buildings, **Mule-Tenders Museum** (open weekends)
0.7	31.6		**Griggstown Lock Area** on right—lock and nature trail
3.4	35.0	R	**Rt. 518** (T; no sign)
0.0	35.0	L	Immediate left onto **canal towpath** (hard-packed dirt)
0.9	35.9	R	At fence, to go to viaduct under Rt. 27. You might wish to walk your bike through here, as it tends to be muddy
0.1	36.0	S	Cross parking lot and road to continue on canal towpath, keeping canoe rental building on right
0.3	36.3		**Lake Carnegie** begins on right after dam. Watch for Princeton University rowing teams!
2.0	38.3		Cross Millstone Aqueduct footbridge
0.4	38.7	R	**Harrison St.** (go **straight** to **Washington Rd.** and turn **left** if you are headed to the **Princeton Junction train station**)
1.1	39.8	S	Cross Nassau St. at traffic light
0.2	40.0	L	**Hamilton Ave.** (traffic light)
0.5	40.5	R	**Moore St.**
0.2	40.7	R	**Houghton St.**
0.1	40.8	L	Into **Princeton High School** parking lot. End of route

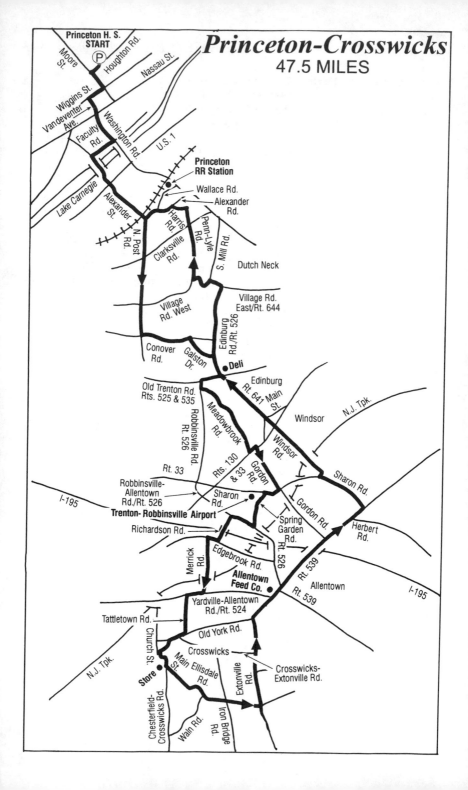

Princeton-Crosswicks—47.5 miles

This route shares some roads with "The New Flat Century." The roads are generally flat and traverse countryside that is fairly undeveloped.

Terrain: Flat, with an occasional rolling hill near a stream valley.

Traffic: Light to moderate. Washington Road is a heavily traveled street leaving Princeton.

Road Conditions: Smooth, for the most part. Some of the more remote back roads and some streets in Princeton have potholes to watch for.

Points of Interest: Trenton-Robbinsville Airport (road goes by end of runway); **Crosswicks** (historic town with pretty homes, churches and a store that serves breakfast and lunch); **Allentown** (a larger historic town containing antique stores in an old mill and a pretty lake with a park).

South of Princeton housing developments and office parks are springing up rapidly, but there's still plenty of great rural Central Jersey terrain to be cycled. Flat to gently rolling roads passing open fields, woods, and streams are the rule on this route. Two pretty old towns, Crosswicks and Allentown, invite you to leave the saddle, explore, and take pictures.

The burgeoning real estate development along the Route 1 corridor is evident for the first few miles of this ride. The development quiets down a bit once you reach the crossroads settlement of Edinburg, where a deli is available.

Travel past the end of the runway of Trenton-Robbinsville Airport for a close-up view of small planes taking off. Then ride to Crosswicks. There are many turns on this part of the route, but to ease the confusion, remember that the turns alternate left-right-left-right.

Stop at Crosswicks for a lunch in the delightful general store/cafe, or just enjoy this pretty, quiet village of old, white houses and large trees. Next, cycle through lush horse farm country to Allentown. There are many interesting shops here, including a group of antique stores in an old gristmill (complete with very slanty wood floors!).

Return to Edinburg on the very quiet Windsor Road, then cycle back to Princeton by way of the pretty community of Dutch Neck.

Directions to Starting Point: Princeton High School is several blocks from the Princeton business district. From U.S. 1, exit at Washington Road/Princeton/Hightstown/Routes 526 and 571. Follow Washington Road into Princeton. Cross Nassau Street/Route 27 just past the University (1.5 miles from Route 1). You will be on Vandeventer Avenue. Turn right at the stop sign onto Wiggins Street, then turn left in several blocks onto Moore Street. A right on Houghton Road as you reach the high school brings you to a parking lot (on the left), where the ride begins.

Train riders: Cross to northbound platform and ride out to Wallace Road. Turn right, then turn right again at Alexander Road. Turn left onto North Post Road and pick up the route at Mile 4.4.

Pt.-Pt.	Cume	Turn	Street/Landmark
0.0	0.0	R	**Houghton Rd.**
0.1	0.1	L	**Moore St.** (T)
0.2	0.3	R	**Wiggins St.** (stop sign)
0.2	0.5	L	**Vandeventer Ave.**
0.1	0.6	S	Cross Nassau St. at traffic light onto **Washington Rd.**
0.8	1.4	R	**Faculty Rd.** (traffic light). Turn is just before the bridge over Lake Carnegie
0.5	1.9	L	**Alexander St.** (T)
1.1	3.0	S	Cross U.S. 1 at traffic light
1.4	4.4	R	**North Post Rd.** (T; no street sign)
0.6	5.0	S	Cross Clarksville Rd./Rt. 638 at traffic light
1.5	6.5	S	Cross Village Rd. W. at stop sign
0.6	7.1	L	**Conover Rd.**
1.2	8.3	R	**Galston Dr.**
0.5	8.8	R	**Edinburg Rd.** (T)
0.6	9.4	R	**Old Trenton Rd./Rts. 526 and 535** (traffic light). **Deli** on left before intersection
0.3	9.7	L	**Robbinsville Rd./Rt. 526**
0.5	10.2	L	**Meadowbrook Rd.**
2.2	12.4	L	**Rt. 130** (T)
0.0	12.4	R	Immediate right onto **Gordon Rd.**
1.6	14.0	R	**Sharon Rd.** (stop sign; no street sign)

Pt.-Pt.	Cume	Turn	Street/Landmark
0.5	14.5	L	**Spring Garden Rd. Trenton-Robbinsville Airport** runway on right after turn
1.3	15.8	R	**Robbinsville-Allentown Rd./Rt. 526** (T; no sign)
0.7	16.5	L	**Richardson Rd.**
1.1	17.6	R	**Edgebrook Rd.** (T)
0.2	17.8	L	**Merrick Rd.**
1.8	19.6	R	**Yardville-Allentown Rd.** (T; no sign)
0.2	19.8	L	**Tattletown Rd.**
0.6	20.4	R	**Old York Rd.** (T)
1.2	21.6	L	**Church St.** (T)
0.3	21.9	L	Curve left onto **Main St.**, Crosswicks
0.1	22.0		**Store** on right
0.1	22.1	S	**Ellisdale Rd.** as you leave Crosswicks. Chesterfield-Crosswicks Rd. goes right
3.1	25.2	L	**Extonville Rd.** This is the second left turn, in case the street signs are missing
2.6	27.8	R	**Old York Rd.** (T). Becomes **South Main St.** in Allentown
0.3	29.1		**"Allentown Feed Company"** (antique stores in picturesque old mill) on left. Continue **straight** out of Allentown on **Rt. 539 North**
3.4	32.5	L	**Sharon Rd.** Brown brick house with an old white picket fence on the corner (street is first left turn past Herbert Rd., which comes off to the right)
0.8	33.3	R	At fork onto **Windsor Rd.** Road crosses New Jersey Turnpike
2.2	35.5	S	Cross Rts. 33/130 at traffic light. Road becomes **Rt. 641**
2.4	37.9	S	Onto **Edinburg Rd./Rt. 526** at traffic light. Deli on right after intersection
1.6	39.5	L	**Village Rd. East/Rt. 644**
0.4	39.9	BL	At fork by large church in Dutch Neck onto **Village Rd. West**. Do not take right fork (S. Mill Rd.) toward Princeton
0.7	40.6	R	**Penn-Lyle Rd.**
1.7	42.3	S	Cross Clarksville Rd. onto **Harris Rd.**
0.4	42.7	L	**Alexander Rd.** (T) If you are returning to the **Princeton Junction train station**, turn **right** shortly after this turn onto **Wallace Road**, which leads into the station

Pt.-Pt.	Cume	Turn	Street/Landmark
0.4	43.1	R	To continue on **Alexander Rd.** No street sign! Alexander Rd. crosses railroad overpass
1.4	44.5	S	Cross U.S. 1 at traffic light
1.1	45.6	R	**Faculty Rd.** (traffic light)
0.5	46.1	L	**Washington Rd.** (traffic light)
0.8	46.9	S	Cross Nassau St. onto **Vandeventer Ave.**
0.1	47.0	R	**Wiggins St.** (stop sign)
0.2	47.2	L	**Moore St.**
0.2	47.4	R	**Houghton Rd.**
0.1	47.5	L	Into **Princeton High School** parking lot. End of route

Princeton-Stockton—55.1 miles

Head west of Princeton toward the Delaware River in this route that is packed with places to see and things to do, and beautiful vistas to admire and photograph. But bring your hill-climbing legs! This part of Central Jersey is far from flat.

Terrain: Hilly, subsiding at times to just gently rolling. Flat along the Delaware River, and gently rolling from Washington Crossing back to Princeton.

Traffic: Light heading over to the river. Moderate from Stockton to Lambertville and back to Princeton. Traffic in New Hope can be quite heavy.

Road Conditions: Smoothly paved, for the most part, with one small stretch of dirt road. Towpath options are hard-packed dirt.

Points of Interest: Green Sergeant's covered bridge (last remaining covered bridge in New Jersey); **gorge of the Wickecheoke Creek**; **Prallsville Mills** area of Delaware & Raritan Canal State Park (historic restoration); river towns of **Stockton, Lambertville** and **New Hope, Pa.** (old stone and frame homes, interesting craft and antique stores, canal-boat rides in New Hope); **Washington Crossing State Park** (N.J.) and **Washington Crossing Historic Park** (Pa.); **Delaware & Raritan Canal** (New Jersey side) and **Delaware Canal** (Pennsylvania side), scenic waterways with towpaths on which cycling is allowed, connecting all Delaware River points on this route; spectacular **horse country** west of Princeton.

This challenging tour of northwestern Mercer and southwestern Hunterdon counties includes enough activities to last a week. Start early, bring a camera or sketchpad, and prepare to be overwhelmed by beautiful scenery and historic places. Or, better yet, stay at an inn in Stockton or New Hope and take a couple of days to do this tour.

Head north and west from Princeton toward Sergeantsville. While passing some of the beautiful estates and horse farms of this area, you will encounter a number of tremendous downhills with great views of the hills and valleys ahead (of course, the price you pay will be a few steep uphills). Watch for deer at all times; they don't seem to be spooked by bicycle wheels.

Ringoes and Sergeantsville are both attractive old towns with stone build-ings and stores to satiate your hunger or thirst (the store in Sergeantsville actually has a large sign stating bikers welcome!). West of Sergeantsville at the bottom of a hill is New Jersey's only covered bridge, the Green Sergeant's bridge, named (or so the sign says) for a local resident.

Turn left by the bridge to cycle along Wickecheoke Creek. This creek has carved a beautiful gorge that can be quite deep. The bottom of the road, and the mouth of the creek, is the Delaware River.

Riding along the Delaware, starting at Prallsville Mills, a historic resto-ration where you can link up with the D&R Canal towpath if you prefer dirt to pavement. Stop to explore the interesting towns of Stockton and Lambertville. Cross the bridge to New Hope, Pa. (you must walk your bike on the sidewalk of all Delaware River bridges). The tour gives you a general outlook of New Hope, which has a high volume of traffic on the weekends. You might wish to lock your bike and explore on foot the town's many interesting shops and old buildings. This alone could take the better part of the day. The mule-drawn canalboat ride is particularly popular with auto tourists.

Next, cycle south to Titusville, a small picture-postcard river hamlet bypassed by the highway. Cross again to Pennsylvania to Washington Crossing Historic Park. Tours of the historic buildings here are avail-able. Its fame stems from General Washington's 1776 Christmas cross-ing of the icy river to retake New Jersey from the British. The Visitor's Center has an interesting film portraying the crossing, and a reproduc-tion of the famous painting of the heroic general in front of the boat hangs on the wall.

Retrace the general's route (using the bridge) by crossing back to New Jersey. It's a relatively flat and short jaunt back to Princeton on moder-ately traveled roads with wide shoulders.

Directions to Starting Point: Princeton High School is several blocks from the Princeton business district. From U.S. 1, exit at Washington Road/Princeton/Hightstown/Routes 526 and 571. Follow Washington Road into Princeton. Cross Nassau Street/Route 27 just past the Uni-versity (1.5 miles from Route 1). You will be on Vandeventer Avenue. Turn right at the stop sign onto Wiggins Street, then turn left in several blocks onto Moore Street. A right on Houghton Road as you reach the high school brings you to a parking lot (on the left), where the ride begins.

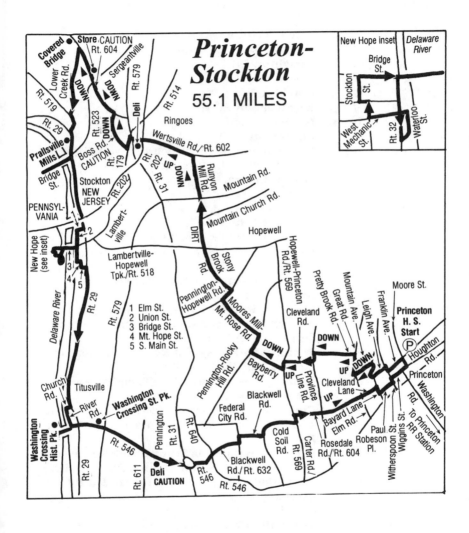

Princeton-
Stockton
55.1 MILES

Train riders: From Princeton Junction's southbound platform, ride through the parking lot and out to Washington Road. Pedal 3 miles to Nassau Street in Princeton then follow the car directions onto Vandeventer Avenue and on to the starting point.

Pt.-Pt.	Cume	Turn	Street/Landmark
0.0	0.0	R	Exit high school parking lot and turn right on **Houghton Rd.**
0.1	0.1	R	**Moore St.** (T)
0.1	0.2	L	**Franklin Ave.**
0.2	0.4	R	**Witherspoon St.** (T)
0.1	0.5	L	**Leigh Ave.**
0.4	0.9	R	**Bayard Lane** (T)
0.1	1.0	BR	Into jughandle marked Mountain Ave./Bayard Lane. Go straight at traffic light onto **Mountain Ave.**
0.7	1.7	R	**Great Rd.** (T)
0.4	2.1	L	**Pretty Brook Rd.**
1.7	3.8	L	**Province Line Rd.** (T)
0.1	3.9	R	**Cleveland Rd.** (no street sign! Turn is an immediate right by a house with a modern-looking "silo")
1.2	5.1	L	**Hopewell-Princeton Rd./Rt. 569** (stop sign; no street sign)
0.6	5.7	SR	**Bayberry Rd.** (turn is in the middle of a curve; you will not see the street sign until after you have made the sharp right)
1.6	7.3	R	**Pennington-Rocky Hill Rd.** (T; no street sign)
0.6	7.9	L	**Moores Mill-Mt. Rose Rd.**
1.9	9.8	R	**Pennington-Hopewell Rd.** (T; no street sign)
0.3	10.1	L	**Stony Brook Rd.**
1.5	11.6	S	Cross unmarked Lambertville-Hopewell Tpk. at stop sign. Continue on unmarked **Stony Brook Rd.**
1.7	13.3	BL	At fork to continue on **Stony Brook Rd.**, which becomes dirt. Mountain Church Rd. goes right
0.7	14.0	S	Cross Mountain Rd. onto **Runyon Mill Rd.** Pavement returns. Watch your speed on incredible downhill ahead
1.4	15.4	L	**Wertsville Rd./Rt. 602** (T; no street sign)
2.3	17.7	S	Cross Rt. 202 at traffic light
0.3	18.0	L	**Rts. 579/179** (T in downtown Ringoes). **Deli** on left at corner

Pt.-Pt.	Cume	Turn	Street/Landmark
0.1	18.1	BR	**Rt. 179 South**
0.0	18.1	R	Immediate right onto the very narrow **Boss Rd.**
1.0	19.1		Use caution at very bumpy railroad crossing
0.5	19.6	L	**Rt. 604** (T; no street sign)
3.4	23.0	S	Cross Rt. 523 at stop sign in downtown Sergeantsville to continue on **Rt. 604 West**. **Store** on right after intersection. SLOW DOWN when you see the 11-foot-3 clearance sign, as the next turn follows shortly
1.2	24.2	L	Onto unmarked **Lower Creek Rd.**, which is just before the **Green Sergeant's covered bridge**. Ride through gorge of the Wickecheoke Creek
2.7	26.9	BL	**Rt. 519** (T; no street sign)
0.2	27.1	BL	**Rt. 29 South** toward Lambertville (stop sign)
0.2	27.3		**Prallsville Mills Historic Area** (Delaware & Raritan Canal State Park) on right. Access to canal towpath at south end of area
0.4	27.7	R	Toward Center Bridge and Solebury on unmarked **Bridge St.**, the main street of **Stockton**. Delis and restaurants are available in Stockton
0.1	27.8		Good outdoor lunch spot by bridge over the river (on canal towpath). Then U-turn and ride back through Stockton
0.1	27.9	R	**Rt. 29 South**
3.0	30.9	R	**Elm St.** (just past fire station as you enter Lambertville)
0.2	31.1	L	**Union St.** (first stop sign; no street sign)
0.5	31.6	R	**Bridge St.** (traffic light). WALK BIKE on sidewalk on the left side of bridge to Pennsylvania (police will ticket you for riding on bridge)
0.4	32.0	L	**Rt. 32 South** (first traffic light in **New Hope**)
0.4	32.4	L	**Waterloo St.**
0.2	32.6	S	Cross Rt. 32 onto **West Mechanic St.**
0.1	32.7	R	At stop sign, onto unmarked street
0.1	32.8	L	At stop sign
0.0	32.8	R	Immediate right onto **Stockton St.** (paralleling railroad tracks)
0.1	32.9	R	**Bridge St.**
0.1	33.0	S	Cross Rt. 32. WALK BIKES on sidewalk on right side of bridge back to New Jersey

Pt.-Pt.	Cume	Turn	Street/Landmark
0.3	33.3	R	**Union St.** (traffic light)
0.2	33.5	L	Curve left onto **Mt. Hope St.**
0.1	33.6	R	**South Main St.** (stop sign)
0.1	33.7	S	Merge onto **Rt. 29 South**
5.7	39.4	R	At traffic light onto unmarked **Church Rd.**, heading into Titusville
0.1	39.5	L	**River Rd.** (T)
0.8	40.3	S	Enter **Washington Crossing State Park**
0.3	40.6	R	At T, walking bikes across bridge into Pennsylvania
0.3	40.9		**Washington Crossing Historic Park** on right. Then U-turn and recross river into New Jersey, walking bikes on sidewalk
0.3	41.2	S	Cross Rt. 29 at traffic light onto **Rt. 546 East** toward Pennington
1.4	42.6	S	Cross Rt. 579 at traffic light
2.0	44.6	S	Cross Rt. 611 at traffic light
0.9	45.5		**Deli** on right
0.5	46.0		Enter traffic circle at junction of Rt. 31 and CAREFULLY cross traffic to head halfway around circle
0.1	46.1	R	Exit circle to continue on **Rt. 546 East**
0.5	46.6	S	At stop sign onto **Rt. 632/Blackwell Rd.** (Rt. 546 goes right; Rt. 640 goes left)
1.3	47.9	L	**Federal City Rd.** (T)
0.1	48.0	R	**Blackwell Rd.** (first right; may not be marked)
1.0	49.0	L	**Cold Soil Rd.** (T)
1.5	50.5	L	**Carter Rd./Rt. 569** (T; no street sign)
0.4	50.9	R	**Rosedale Rd./Rt. 604** toward Princeton
2.6	53.5	S	Cross Elm Rd. at traffic light onto **Cleveland Lane**
0.6	54.1	R	**Bayard Lane** (T)
0.1	54.2	L	**Paul Robeson Place** (traffic light)
0.3	54.5	S	Cross Witherspoon St. at traffic light onto **Wiggins St.**
0.3	54.8	L	**Moore St.**
0.2	55.0	R	**Houghton Rd.**
0.1	55.1	L	Into **Princeton High School** parking lot. End of route

New Jersey's only remaining covered bridge, Green Sergeant's Covered Bridge is located west of Sergeantsville. It was originally built circa 1750 and rebuilt in 1872. It was dismantled in 1961 to make way for a conventional bridge, but public outcry prompted the state to reconstruct it from the original materials. The name of the bridge comes from Richard Green Sergeant, who lived nearby.

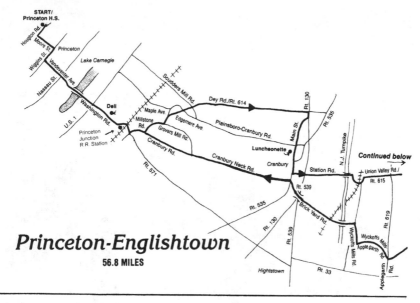

Princeton-Englishtown

56.8 MILES

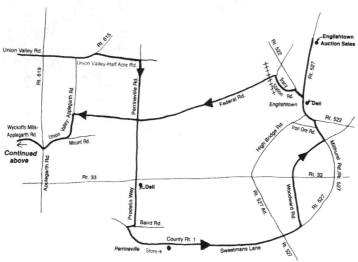

Princeton-Englishtown—56.8 miles

If you don't think you can cycle this distance, you're probably wrong—the only thing that will take you out of high gear is a headwind. Flat is the operative word for this route, which incorporates a few roads from "The New Flat Century."

Terrain: Pancake flat for much of the ride. Occasional gently rolling terrain, especially near Perrineville.

Traffic: Moderate in this growing area, except near Princeton, Cranbury, and Englishtown, where it is a bit heavier. On peak flea market days (weekends in summer and fall), you will be cycling faster than the cars.

Road Conditions: Good, to occasionally bumpy on the more remote roads.

Points of Interest: Cranbury (a pretty town with a Main Street lined with old, white frame homes); **Englishtown Auction Sales** (flea market).

Feel cooped up in your office? In need of exercise? Don't want to hassle with hills? This is the ride for you! Cycling fast down long, straight roads with traffic that is tolerable (except in rush hour) is a great stress-reliever and cure for many problems of modern life. The scenery of farmland and woods is easy on the eye as you spin your way east to Englishtown.

Start by cycling out of Princeton to Grovers Mill, a community made famous as a Martian landing site by Orson Wells' 1938 broadcast of *The War Of The Worlds*. The road to Cranbury gives you an idea of what not to expect on this route—there are no curves, there are no hills.

Cranbury is a town out of a 1940s movie with its picturesque Main Street. A park with a lake anchors the town on the south end and is a good place for a picnic.

Next cycle along County Route 1, which gently rolls through prime farm country, with orchards prevalent. Head north through horse farms into Englishtown. The flea market here is world-famous and occupies many acres. Bring a sturdy lock if you plan to explore the bargains.

The return to Princeton is a direct route and does not pass through any towns, so be sure to stock up on food and water before leaving Englishtown.

Directions to Starting Point: Princeton High School is several blocks from the Princeton business district. From U.S. 1, exit at Washington Road/Princeton/Hightstown/Routes 526 and 571. Follow Washington Road into Princeton. Cross Nassau Street/Route 27 just past the University (1.5 miles from Route 1). You will be on Vandeventer Ave. Turn right at the stop sign onto Wiggins Street, then turn left in several blocks onto Moore Street. A right on Houghton Road as you reach the high school brings you to a parking lot (on the left), where the ride begins.

Train riders: From the southbound Princeton Junction platform, cycle out to Washington Road. Turn right to cross the tracks. This is the turn at Mile 3.5 of the cue sheet.

Pt.-Pt.	Cume	Turn	Street/Landmark
0.0	0.0	R	**Houghton Rd.**
0.1	0.1	L	**Moore St.** (T)
0.2	0.3	R	**Wiggins St.** (stop sign)
0.2	0.5	L	**Vandeventer Ave.**
0.1	0.6	S	Cross Nassau St. at traffic light onto **Washington Rd.**
1.7	2.3	S	Cross U.S. 1 at traffic light
0.5	2.8		**Deli** on left
0.7	3.5	L	Turn toward Hightstown and Freehold (you are on **Rts. 526/571**), crossing railroad overpass
0.2	3.7	L	**Rt. 615/Cranbury Rd.** (traffic light) toward Grovers Mill and Cranbury
0.8	4.5	SL	**Millstone Rd.** Road changes name to **Grovers Mill Rd.**
0.8	5.3	L	At traffic light onto **Maple Ave.** (sign says Plainsboro)
0.3	5.6	R	**Edgemere Ave.** (street is hard to find; watch for it)
0.6	6.2	S	Cross Plainsboro Rd. at stop sign onto **Dey Rd.**
0.3	6.5	S	Cross Scudders Mill Rd. at traffic light onto **Rt. 614 East**
4.5	11.0	R	**Rt. 130 South** (traffic light)
0.1	11.1	BR	Bear right immediately toward Cranbury. You will be on **Main St./Rt. 535 South**, though there is no street sign

Pt.-Pt.	Cume	Turn	Street/Landmark
1.2	12.3		**Luncheonette** on right
0.5	12.8	L	**Station Rd.** If you come to a fork where Rt. 535 bears right at the junction of Rt. 539, you've gone too far
0.4	13.2	S	Cross Rt. 130 at traffic light onto **Rt. 615 North**
1.2	14.4	L	Curve left to cross railroad tracks
0.1	14.5	L	At T to continue on **Rt. 615 North**
0.9	15.4	S	Cross Rt. 619/Applegarth Rd. at stop sign to continue on **Rt. 615 North/Union Valley Rd.**
1.0	16.4	R	**Union Valley Half Acre Rd.** (by Pondview Plaza). Rt. 615 North goes left
1.0	17.4	R	**Perrineville Rd.** (stop sign; no street sign)
3.0	20.4	S	Cross Rt. 33 at traffic light. **Deli** on left after intersection. Road becomes **Prodelin Way**
2.2	22.6	R	**Baird Rd.** (T; no sign)
0.0	22.6	L	Immediate left onto **Monmouth County Rt. 1** (T) (no sign). Becomes **Perrineville Rd.**
1.3	23.9		**Ray's Deli** on right. Road will change name to **Sweetmans Lane**
3.6	27.5	S	At junction of Rt. 527 onto **Rt. 527 North/ Sweetmans Lane**
0.2	27.7	L	**Woodward Rd.**
1.3	29.0	S	Cross Rt. 33 at stop sign
2.2	31.2	L	**Millhurst Rd./Rt. 527** (stop sign)
1.6	32.8	L	At T to continue on **Rt. 527 North** (no signs)
0.3	33.1		**Deli** on right in downtown Englishtown
1.4	34.5		**Englishtown Auction Sales** (flea market) on right. Then U-turn and return the way you came (on **Rt. 527 South**)
1.1	35.6	R	**Rt. 522 East**
0.2	35.8	BL	Onto unmarked **Tracy Station Rd.** (toward Englishtown Commons). Turn is where Rt. 522 curves right
1.2	37.0	S	Road changes name to **Federal Rd.** Tracy Station Rd. goes right. Street sign may be turned around. Federal Rd. curves left after this intersection and crosses a railroad grade crossing in 0.3 miles
3.5	40.5	S	Cross Perrineville Rd. at stop sign
1.3	41.8	L	**Union Valley-Applegarth Rd.** (T; no street sign)
0.6	42.4	R	At T to continue on **Union Valley-Applegarth Rd.** Mount Rd. goes left

Pt.-Pt.	Cume	Turn	Street/Landmark
0.7	43.1	**R-BL**	Turn **right** on unmarked **Applegarth Rd.** at stop sign and **bear left** immediately onto unmarked **Wyckoffs Mills-Applegarth Rd.** This is a very narrow road.
1.0	44.1	**R**	**Wyckoffs Mills Rd.** Road goes under high tension wires shortly. If you cross a river, you've missed the turn
0.5	44.6	**L**	At unmarked intersection onto **Brick Yard Rd.** You will pass a horse farm on right. Road will cross N.J. Turnpike
1.8	46.4	**S**	Cross Rt. 130 at traffic light onto **Rt. 539 North** toward Cranbury
1.0	47.4	**L**	**Cranbury Neck Rd.** If you enter downtown Cranbury, you've gone too far. Road will change name to **Cranbury Rd.** as you approach Princeton Junction and becomes **Rt. 615 South**
5.7	53.1	**R**	**Hightstown Rd./Rts. 526 and 571** (traffic light). Cross railroad overpass
0.2	53.3	**BR**	**Washington Rd.**, toward Princeton (turn **left** here for **Princeton Junction train station**)
0.7	54.0		**Deli** on right
0.5	54.5	**S**	Cross U.S. 1 at traffic light
1.7	56.2	**S**	Cross Nassau St. at traffic light onto **Vandeventer Ave.**
0.1	56.3	**R**	**Wiggins St.** (stop sign)
0.2	56.5	**L**	**Moore St.** (T)
0.2	56.7	**R**	**Houghton Rd.**
0.1	56.8	**L**	Into **Princeton High School** parking lot. End of route

About The Author

Dan Goldfischer is the originator of the *RIDE GUIDE* series of bicycle guidebooks, beginning in 1985 with *RIDE GUIDE for North Jersey and Beyond.* The original book was split into two volumes, one for North Jersey and one for Central Jersey.

Dan has been biking and writing in New Jersey for 20 years. Besides bicycle guidebooks, Dan wrote the "25 Great Hikes in Morris County" series for *The Daily Record* and is the newspaper's transportation columnist.

ORDER THESE ANACUS PRESS BICYCLE GUIDES!

RIDE GUIDE/North Jersey (2nd edition), by Dan Goldfischer ($14.95). Visit the rural northwest corner of the state, cycle through the unspoiled Great Swamp near Basking Ridge, or follow one of the more urban routes near the George Washington Bridge.

RIDE GUIDE/Central Jersey (2nd edition), by Dan Goldfischer ($14.95). Twenty-six rides, including four new hybrid routes, showcase the best of Somerset, Hunterdon, Mercer, Middlesex, Monmouth, and Ocean counties. Most rides in this area are flat to gently rolling, with few steep climbs.

RIDE GUIDE/South Jersey (2nd edition), by Alex and Nancy May ($12.95). Bicyclists look to South Jersey for its flat terrain, rural, undeveloped farmlands, and forest preserves. This Ride Guide contains 26 routes in the eight southern counties of New Jersey, passing by the Atlantic Ocean, Delaware Bay, and through the Pine Barrens.

RIDE GUIDE/New Jersey Mountain Biking, by Joshua Pierce ($14.95). A selection of the best off-road trails in the state, from sea level at the shore to the mountains of the Skylands. Mountain bikers of all skill levels will appreciate the detailed maps and cue sheets and notes on topography, trail conditions, and points of interest.

RIDE GUIDE/Mountain Biking in the New York Metro Area, by Joel Sendek ($14.95). Mountain bikers stuck in Manhattan and its environs will find everything they need to get out of the concrete canyons and onto some of the best trails in the tri-state area. Detailed directions to most of the trails via mass transit are provided, and all are within a reasonable drive. Maps, cue sheets, and notes on topography, trail conditions, and points of interest round out this invaluable volume.

RIDE GUIDE/Hudson Valley New Paltz to Staten Island (2nd edition), by Dan Goldfischer ($10.95). Directions via Metro North to some of the 29 rides (including 4 off-road) in this book make it the ideal guide for those city-bound New Yorkers who want to escape to the country or ride close to home.

Bed, Breakfast and Bike/Mid-Atlantic, by Alex and Nancy May ($14.95). The Mays take you from the Finger Lakes and Adirondacks of New York through Pennsylvania's Amish country and Bucks County, "down the shore" in New Jersey, Delaware, Maryland and Virginia into the hills of West Virginia.

Bed, Breakfast and Bike/Pacific Northwest, by Carrie and Jon Muellner ($14.95). Mountains, seashore, farmlands and rain forest—the area from British Columbia to Oregon offers cyclists a little bit of everything. 32 bike-friendly inns are described.

Please send me these books:

Qty.	Title	Amount
	Shipping	$2.00
	NJ residents please add 6% sales tax	
	Total	

Send books to:

Name:_____

Address:_____

City/State/Zip/Country:_____

Send coupon and payment to:

ANACUS
PRESS INC.
P.O. Box 4544, Warren, NJ 07059